THE ROAD TO WAR
1933–1939

Ross Mackintosh

D0183380

ANDREW HUNT

Hodder Gibson

A MEMBER OF THE HODDER HEADLINE GROUP

Orders: please contact Bookpoint Ltd, 130 Milton Park, Abingdon, Oxon OX14 4SB. Telephone: (44) 01235 827720, Fax: (44) 01235 400454. Lines are open from 9.00–6.00, Monday to Saturday, with a 24 hour message answering service.
You can also order through our website www.hoddereducation.co.uk

British Library Cataloguing in Publication Data
A catalogue record for this title is available from The British Library

ISBN-10: 0-340-77477-0
ISBN-10: 978-0-340-77477-9

Published by Hodder Gibson, 2a Christie Street, Paisley. PA1 1NB
Tel: 0141 848 1609. Fax: 0141 889 6315. E-mail: hoddergibson@hodder.co.uk

First published 2000
Impression number   10   9   8   7   6   5   4
Year   2006   2005

Cover photo: **Hitler in open car greeting, during Reichs Party Convention (Reichparteitag) in Nuremburg, 1936,** AKG Photo
Typeset by Fakenham Photosetting Limited, Fakenham, Norfolk
Printed in Great Britain for Hodder Gibson, 2a Christie Street, Paisley. PA1 1NB Scotland, UK by Arrowsmith, Bristol.

ACKNOWLEDGEMENTS

The illustrations were drawn by: Hardlines Illustrations and Design; Richard Duszczak Cartoons.

The publishers would like to thank the following individuals, institutions and companies for permission to reproduce photographs in this book:

Bilderdienst Suddeutscher Verlag 14; Daily Express 61 (bottom left); Daily Telegraph 61 (bottom right); David Low, Evening Standard/Centre for Study of Cartoons and Caricatures, University of Kent at Canterbury/© Solo Syndication 17, 39, 52, 56, 65, 75 (top and bottom); Ernest Shepard/Punch Publications 28, 44; Hulton Getty 41, 60, 61 (top); Imperial War Museum 26, 59, 72; Landesbildstelle, Berlin 12; L'Illustration/Sygma 20; Morning Star, London 58; Popperfoto 13, 16, 76; Punch Publications 55.

The publishers would also like to thank the following for permission to reproduce material in this book: Edward Arnold for extracts from *Arms, Autarky and Aggression* by William Carr; Her Majesty's Stationary Office for works published by the Crown and Parliament, including speeches made in The House of Commons; Pimlico for extracts from *Mein Kampf* by Adolf Hitler; The Royal Institute of International Affairs for extracts from *The Speeches of Adolf Hitler, April 1922–August 1939* by Norman Baynes.

Every effort of has been made to trace ownership of copyright. The publishers will be happy to make arrangements with any copyright holder it has not been possible to contact.

CONTENTS

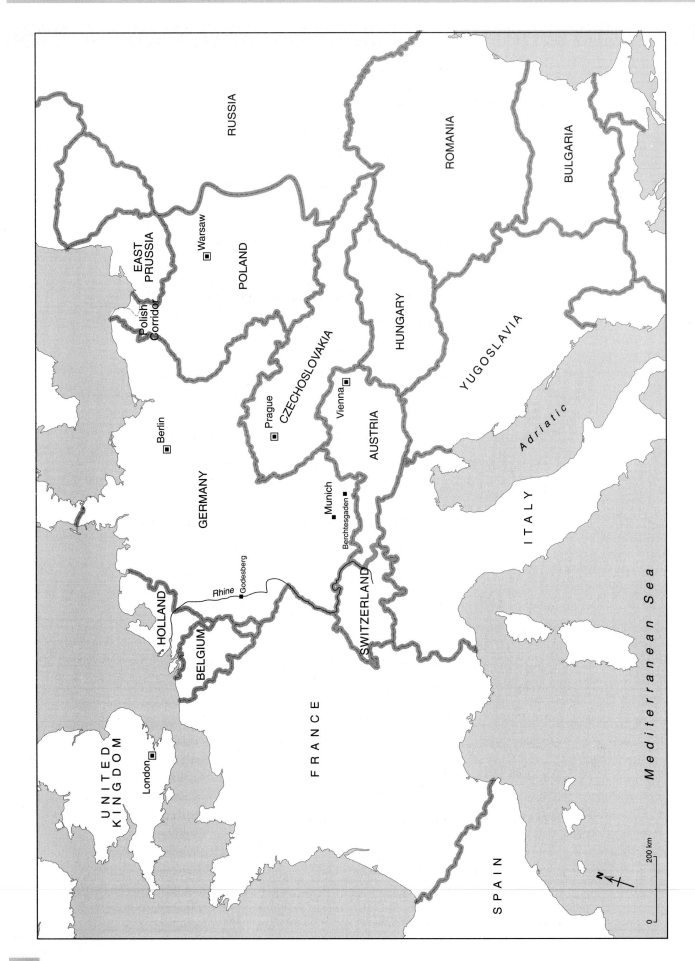

RUSSIA

ROMANIA

BULGARIA

EAST PRUSSIA

Warsaw

POLAND

Polish Corridor

CZECHOSLOVAKIA

HUNGARY

YUGOSLAVIA

Prague

Vienna

Adriatic

Berlin

GERMANY

AUSTRIA

ITALY

Munich

Berchtesgaden

Godesberg

Rhine

SWITZERLAND

HOLLAND

BELGIUM

FRANCE

Mediterranean Sea

UNITED KINGDOM

London

SPAIN

200 km

0

1914–1918	First World War
11 November 1918	Armistice
28 June 1919	Signing of Treaty of Versailles
1920	Creation of Nazi party
February 1920	Nazi Party 25 Point Programme issued
November 1923	Hitler's Munich Putsch
1924	Hitler writes *Mein Kampf* in Landsberg Prison
1925	Locarno Pact
1925–1929	The 'Locarno Years' of friendship among European Powers
1930	The start of the Great Depression
1930–1933	The rise in support for Hitler and Nazi party
1932–1933	Geneva Disarmament Conference
30 January 1933	Hitler becomes Chancellor of Germany
February 1933	Hitler's *Speech to his generals* on foreign policy aims
October 1933	Hitler leaves Geneva Disarmament Conference
January 1934	Polish-German Non-Aggression Pact
July 1934	Austrian Nazis assassinate Chancellor Dollfuss of Austria
January 1935	Saar Plebiscite returns Saarland to Germany
9 March 1935	Hitler admits existence of German airforce (Luftwaffe)
16 March 1935	Hitler introduces conscription to build up army
16 June 1935	Anglo-German Naval Agreement
1935	Peace Ballot showed British public's support for League of Nations
December 1935	Hoare-Laval Pact; an attempt to end Abyssinian Crisis by a deal with Italy
February 1936	France signs Franco-Russian Mutual Assistance Pact
7 March 1936	Germany re-occupies demilitarised zone of Rhineland
July 1936	Austro-German Agreement Spanish Civil War starts
November 1936	Rome-Berlin Axis (deepens friendship between Germany and Italy)
22 April 1937	Bombing of Guernica in Spanish Civil War by German aircraft
November 1937	Hossbach Memorandum Lord Halifax's visit to Germany to set out British policy
February 1938	Austrian Chancellor Schuschnigg visits Hitler in Germany

9 March 1938	Schuschnigg's attempted plebiscite on future of Austria
12 March 1938	German forces invade Austria
13 March 1938	Austrian government declares it is now part of Germany
10 April 1938	Austrian people vote in plebiscite to be part of Germany
April 1938	Sudeten German Party issues the Karlsbad Programme
20–21 May 1938	May Crisis in Czechoslovakia
28 May 1938	Hitler orders 'Case Green' for occupation of Czechoslovakia
July 1938	Runciman mission goes to Czechoslovakia
4 September 1938	President Benes of Czechoslovakia accepts the Karlsbad Programme
13 September 1938	Hitler's Nuremberg speech criticising President Benes
15 September 1938	Chamberlain's visit to Berchtesgaden to meet Hitler
22 September 1938	Chamberlain's flight to Godesberg to meet Hitler
25 September 1938	Masaryk's note to Chamberlain saying Czechs will fight
26 September 1938	Chamberlain's radio speech to British people on closeness of war (trying on gas masks etc.)
29 September 1938	Munich Conference divides up Czechoslovakia
15 March 1939	German forces occupy the rest of western Czechoslovakia (Bohemia-Moravia). Slovakia (the eastern end) asks to become a protectorate
31 March 1939	Anglo-Polish Alliance. Britain promises to defend Poland
April 1939	Hitler orders 'Case White', the plans for invasion of Poland
23 August 1939	Molotov-Ribbentrop Pact between Germany and Russia.
	Russia and Germany agree to carve up Poland between them
1 September 1939	Hitler invades Poland
3 September 1939	Chamberlain's radio broadcast to the British nation that Britain is at war with Germany.
September 1939–May 1945	Second World War

INTRODUCTION

When the fighting of the Great War ended at the Armistice in November 1918, and the Peace Treaties were signed in the chateaux outside Paris in 1919, most people in Europe would have believed that they had indeed fought 'the War to end all wars'. They believed the following decades would be a time of recovery, reconstruction and a new world-order of peace. Some peered anxiously ahead, wondering how it would all turn out, but for most it was a time of hope and thankfulness.

Yet only 20 years later, in September 1939, a second, even more destructive war started, largely between the same sides as the first. Its causes seemed to lie very much in *unfinished business*, the fact that the Peace Treaties of 1919 had caused new problems rather than solving old ones. This was especially true of the way Germany had been humiliated through the harsh terms of the Treaty of Versailles. It was Germany's attempts through the 1920s and 30s to recover her pride, then her strength and territory, that led to the outbreak of the Second World War. It could be argued then that the Second World War was really just 'The Great War: Part 2'.

It would be wrong however to regard history as an inevitable sequence of pre-ordained events. After all, if this was the case, politicians wouldn't ever bother trying to solve disputes since their actions would make no difference in the end. Surely then, there must have been choices that could have been made, turning points when intelligence could have been applied to the situation, or opportunities taken to avoid an outbreak of war.

The topic heading for the Intermediate 1 and 2 unit on European inter-war diplomacy is entitled *The Road to War 1933–39*. This title rather suggests that it was a pretty inevitable course of events; but was it a road heading straight to disaster, or was it a road with plenty of signposts pointing the way to peace with plenty of chances to follow those directions? Remember, for anybody living in the 1920s and 30s, there was no such concept as *inter-war*, they didn't see themselves as merely living in a small historical break between two great wars. From their viewpoint, *nothing* inevitably led anywhere (at least until the last moments before the outbreak of war itself) and they always felt they had choices about what foreign policy to follow without assuming it only led to war.

This is part of the fascination and intrigue of this topic in history and makes it so worth studying today. After all, it was only three generations ago, in a European geographical area we are roughly familiar with, and with participants who shared recognisably similar features to the nations of today (ambition and pride for individuals, honour for one's country, desire for power or peace, ability to show aggression or compromise and self sacrifice). All of these uncertain and variable factors were combined with the unsettled conditions in 1930s Europe. From this point of view, it would be pretty hard to argue that it was all leading to an inevitable second great war.

So, in your study of this unit, analyse it bit by bit, break it down into the important questions that need to be considered, and then see what is involved in each event or idea. See how it adds up over the study of the whole unit. You may think that many of the 'bits' do seem to fit together into a sort of path to war, but that often has more to do with the way historians try and explain the past than the actions of the participants at the time. Don't patronise them by saying to yourself *How could they have been so stupid, couldn't they see that everything was leading to war?* because, to them, it wasn't.

The Road to War 1933–1939 unit outline requires you to study all the following areas: *German foreign policy before the Second World War, Nazi ideas, anger at the Versailles Treaty, re-armament, re-occupation of the Rhineland, Anschluss with Austria. Czechoslovakia and the Munich Crisis. The reaction of Britain and France, their policy of appeasement and its effectiveness.*

These topics have been broken down into chapters that make sense, and each chapter has both **What do you think?** sections within it, and **Question Practice** sections in the middle and/or at the end. The **What do you think?** sections cover key points for discussion, to help you check that you have understood the text so far.

NAZISM: ITS PRINCIPLES AND IDEAS

This chapter will do four main things:

◆ look at the background to the rise of Hitler and the Nazi Party
◆ discuss the importance of *racism* in Hitler's doctrines
◆ look at the policy of *lebensraum*
◆ consider the Treaty of Versailles and its impact on Germany and its politics

INTRODUCTION

Any attempt to explain the twisty path of European *diplomacy* in the 1930s can only properly do so by getting into the minds of the leading players. The events did not just happen, they do not explain themselves; they were the product of someone's planning. We must ask ourselves what the planners were trying to achieve and why?

Hitler was one of the leading players. During the 1920s, the years following Germany's defeat in the First World War, Hitler began expressing his views about the future course of foreign policy that Germany should take. The views he held as an individual seemed to continue as he became the leader of the Nazi Party in 1920, then *Chancellor* of Germany in 1933, and then *Fuhrer* of the German Reich from 1934 onwards. To understand the way that foreign policy developed under Hitler's direction, we must look at some of the principles of Nazi *ideology* that he had drawn up.

THE BACKGROUND TO THE RISE OF THE NAZI PARTY

In the years following the ending of the Great War, many small political parties were being set up throughout Germany, as the German people debated what political direction Germany should take in the future. Although Hitler had been gassed during the last months of the war and was recovering in hospital at the time of the *Armistice* in November 1918, by the middle of 1919 he was being employed by the army in its Press and News Bureau. His job was to check out the new small political parties (Munich alone had about 50), to see if they favoured communism or were encouraging socialism or pacifism among the returning soldiers. Hitler went to visit one party, called the German Workers Party, and realised he could take it over, build it up and make it follow the policies that he wanted it to. He could use it as a means to achieve political power.

He re-named the party, calling it the National Socialist German Workers Party (Nazi Party) and he drew up the party's official 25 point *programme*. The first four points dealt with foreign policy, the next five with the Jews, and the remainder chiefly with economic and welfare issues. It is in this document that we can see the points which became the basics of the main foreign policy issues that concerned Hitler for the rest of his life.

SOURCE 1.1

THE OFFICIAL PROGRAMME OF THE NAZI PARTY

1 We demand the union of all Germans to form a Great Germany by the right of self-determination of peoples.
2 We demand equality of rights of the German people in its dealing with other nations and abolition of the Peace Treaties of Versailles and St Germain.
3 We demand land and territories (colonies) to provide food for our people and to settle our extra population.
4 None but those of German blood may be citizens of the state. No Jew can therefore be a member of the nation.
8 All non-German immigration must be stopped
10 It must be the first duty of each citizen of the state to work with his mind or with his body. The needs of an individual must not clash with the interests of the state, but must go on within the framework of the community (Volksgemeinschaft) and be for the general good of everybody.
22 We demand abolition of a paid army and the formation of a national army.

These policy statements showed that Hitler and the Nazis were a right-wing *nationalist* party and were opposed to democratic government.

WHAT DO YOU THINK?

What is there about the 1920 Nazi party programme that shows that Hitler was a German nationalist?

WHAT DO YOU THINK?

Considering just the information written in the paragraph on the right and Source 1.2, can you suggest what strengths and weaknesses *Mein Kampf* would have as a source for any historian studying German foreign policy in the 1930s?

Hitler demonstrated his anti-democratic beliefs in November 1923, when at the height of the German inflation crisis, he started an armed uprising known as the *Munich Putsch* . He planned to gather support, march on Berlin and topple the existing democratic government (known as the Weimar Government). His putsch failed, he was arrested, tried and imprisoned. During the eight months that he was in Landsberg prison, he had time to think. This let him develop and explain his political ideas, which he then put into print in his book *Mein Kampf* (My Struggle). This is the second significant document that must be studied to come to an understanding of Hitler's beliefs. As the historian William Carr wrote:

SOURCE 1.2

'... it does not seem unreasonable to assume that the thoughts this strange man committed to paper ... at the age of 36 probably represented sincerely-held beliefs from which he did not deviate...'

During the period from 1924–29, Hitler and the Nazi party had little electoral or popular success. Germany began to make an economic recovery after the Great Inflation of 1923, and the democratic government of Germany gradually moved towards a better understanding with the Allied governments. This was an age of *rapprochement*, and the Nazis with their extremist ideas were regarded as little more than cranks. The economic down-turn associated with the *Great Depression* from 1930, dramatically altered the picture for Hitler and the Nazi Party. With the democratic parties so dismally failing to prop up the struggling German economy, more Germans now seemed prepared to listen to those with extreme political views, who claimed they had the solution to Germany's problems. Hitler and the Nazis began to get more votes; by 1932 they were the largest party in the *Reichstag* and by 1933 Hitler was invited to become Chancellor of Germany. The democratic process had put into power a would-be dictator, a man who only ten years earlier had tried to take power by an armed uprising! The principles and doctrines that he had been nurturing over the previous decade would now become the actual policy of the German government.

THE IMPORTANCE OF RACISM IN HITLER'S DOCTRINES

A look at the 1920 Nazi Party programme perhaps highlights the German nationalist flavour of Hitler's policies. It spells out what will happen to Germans inside Germany, and it is anti-Jewish, but it does not give actual details of what might happen to other races outside Germany's borders, or how this might influence Germany's broader foreign policy. The 1920 Programme also says very little about Hitler's hatred of Communism, yet this also was at the heart of what Nazism stood for.

It is only when we look at *Mein Kampf* that some of the full effects of Hitler's policies begin to show themselves. As William Carr put it, it is then that we appreciate that:

SOURCE 1.3

'Hitler's foreign policy can only be properly understood as an expression of his racial beliefs.'

Hitler's statements on race can be found throughout *Mein Kampf*. He believed in a crude Social Darwinism. This theory claimed that human life was little different from that of wild animals in the jungle. Life was a struggle where only the fittest races deserved to survive. Hitler wrote:

SOURCE 1.4

'The question of race is the key to world history ... in that relentless struggle for existence, which is the law of life, the Aryan (German) race, has emerged as the master-people (Herrenvolk).'

He believed that since the German people were a superior race, then its racial mission must be to conquer the world. Hitler's first duty, to help Germany fulfil its 'racial mission', would be to bring all people of German blood within the one state.

WHAT DO YOU THINK?

How important was race to Hitler in his overall policies. Explain and support your answer.

THE POLICY OF LEBENSRAUM

The policy of *Lebensraum* can be seen as an obvious consequence of the racial policies that Hitler believed in. Once all those of German blood outside Germany (*Auslandsdeutsch*) had been brought into the German *Reich* (Point 3 of the 1920 Nazi Programme), then Germany would not be big enough to hold them. Self-preservation meant that the German people would need more space, and the racial superiority Hitler claimed for the German people meant they would be entitled to expand eastwards into regions that Hitler said were *'ripe for dissolution'* and to exploit the resources there. He believed that the struggle for living space (*Lebensraum*) would be one of the main features of German foreign policy in the coming years. He wrote:

SOURCE 1.5

'One must calmly and squarely face the truth that it certainly cannot have been God's will to give fifty times more land to one nation than another ... If this earth has sufficient room for all, then we ought to have a big enough share to meet all our needs.'

It was not in Hitler's mind to look towards the west for this 'living space'. He didn't want to threaten the Western democracies (UK, France) who he believed would fall into line behind him once they saw the success of his policies. The areas where Hitler thought living space was available were all east of Germany and included Poland, Czechoslovakia, the small Baltic states and then European Russia and the Ukraine. The historian William Carr wrote:

SOURCE 1.6

'When looked at from this wider view, joining all the Germans together into the German fatherland has lesser importance, and getting back German Austria and taking the Sudetenland were only steps on the road to the real goal. This was to make Germany the dominant power in Europe at the expense of the racially inferior peoples in the east.'

So, what we see with Hitler's racial and *Lebensraum* policies is something of the long-term view. They were a part of the Nazi ideology that he held, and therefore were aims to be achieved, but they could not come about overnight. Other things stood in the way of his racial and imperial dream, chiefly the terms of the 1919 Treaty of Versailles, which seemed to have demolished Germany's hopes of international power forever. It was the dismantling of the terms of Versailles which would have to become the more immediate short-term aim of Hitler's foreign policy.

WHAT DO YOU THINK?

1. Study Hitler's own words. How does he justify the policy of *Lebensraum*?
2. Explain why the 'racial mission' and *Lebensraum* had to be *long term* goals of Nazi foreign policy.

THE TREATY OF VERSAILLES AND ITS IMPACT ON GERMANY AND ITS POLITICS

Hitler always referred to the 1919 Treaty of Versailles as a *Diktat*, a dictated peace forced upon a helpless Germany. He saw the harshness of its terms as an opportunity; he could whip up the hatred of the German people against it and they would put him into power. Hitler said:

SOURCE 1.7

'Each one of the points of that Treaty could be burnt into the minds and hearts of the German people until 60 million men and women find their souls aflame with a feeling of rage and shame; and a torrent of fire bursts forth as from a furnace, and a will of steel is forged from it, with the common cry – "We will be strong again!"'

Hitler was able to complain about the harsh effect of every aspect of the terms of the Treaty. He appreciated that this would be a popular platform for the Nazis to use to gain votes, and this led it to appear as Points 1 and 2 of the 1920 Nazi programme.

Briefly, the main terms of Versailles that affected Germany were:

◆ *The Territorial terms:* Germany had lost land in the east to Poland, France had insisted on a de-militarised Rhineland and also taken the Saarland for 15 years as a guarantee of future payment of reparations. Germany had been forbidden to join with Austria, and new states had been created (like Czechoslovakia) which contained substantial German minorities.

◆ *The Military terms:* Germany's army was reduced to 100 000 men with no short-service conscription, it was permitted no heavy artillery, tanks or poison gas. Germany was to have no military airforce or submarines and a small naval fleet with only six warships of 10 000 tons.

◆ *The Financial terms:* Germany had to accept a reparations bill of £6 600 000 000 in 1921, to pay for the damage caused to the Allies. This had been revised in 1924 (Dawes Plan) then revised again (Young Plan) in 1929 to stretch the payment by 60 years.

◆ *The War Guilt Clause;* Germany had no choice but to sign Article 231 of the Treaty which said that Germany alone accepted the blame for having caused the war.

For 13 years, Hitler used arguments for the abolition of all these harsh and vindictive terms of the Treaty of Versailles as the main short-term aim of his foreign policy. Getting Versailles out of the way would clear the decks for the bigger ideas that he had in mind. As Carr wrote, about Hitler's cynical use of the Versailles issue:

SOURCE 1.8

'... the need to win and keep mass support during his rise to power in the early 1930s influenced the foreign policy Hitler preached in public. The resentment and frustration of the masses had to be directed against an easily identifiable target. Attacks on the Treaty of Versailles plus appeals for all German speaking people to

be joined into one state, never failed to arouse enthusiasm in audiences which were used to the idea that Germany had been treated shabbily in 1919.'

SOURCE 1.9 *A Nazi propaganda cartoon shows Germany's army, limited by the Versailles treaty, surrounded by hostile neighbours*

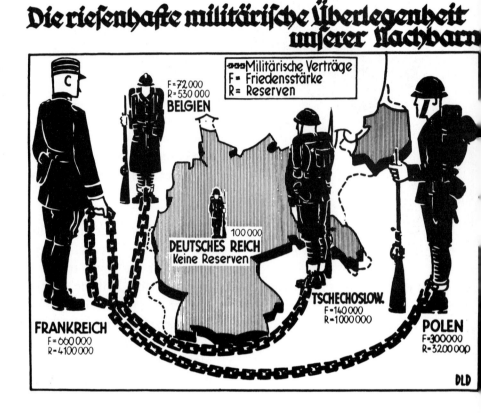

Any attempt, therefore, to explain German foreign policy in the 1930s, once Hitler and the Nazi Party had come to power, must keep the following points in mind:

1 There was a short-term policy to remove the terms of Versailles which placed restrictions on Germany. This might take ten years or more to achieve, but would be very popular with the German people. Success in the short-term strategy would lead to success in the long-term strategy because:
 ◆ it would make Germany stronger
 ◆ it would remove new states in Eastern Europe which stood in the way of the longer term plans
2 There was a longer-term policy which was racial and territorial. It was chiefly aimed at gaining territory in the east at the expense of 'inferior races'. This strategy would lead to Jews being exterminated, Slavic races being turned into a slave-labour force and Communism being crushed. New economic resources would become available to Germany, which would strengthen its people and help develop the 'Master Race'.

HITLER'S FOREIGN POLICY AIMS

Revenge for the Treaty of Versailles and abolish its terms

Build up the Master Race and prove German racial superiority

Hitler's ideas in Mein Kampf

Return all Germans outside Germany to their German homeland

Lebensraum
Fight to get the extra living space that Germany needed

SOURCE 1.10 *'Mr Respectable' Adolf Hitler as the new German Chancellor greets President Hindenburg*

When these Nazi policies are just baldly written down, the temptation is to say '*Blimey, they're the ravings of a madman*', but don't be deceived; these were the main foreign policy aims that Hitler and the Nazi Party set out to achieve in their 12 years in power. They may well have been the ravings of a madman, but once Hitler became Chancellor of Germany in January 1933, they were going to be German foreign policy nevertheless.

QUESTION PRACTICE

*i*1

(See pages 93–99 for advice on different types of questions)

SOURCE 1.11 From the Nazi Party 25 point programme.

[Point 3] We demand land and territories (colonies) to provide food for our people and to settle our extra population.

1 What were the foreign policy ideas of the Nazis?

(Outcome 1 – 3 marks)

(Use the source and recalled knowledge)

SOURCE 1.12 Hitler writing in *Mein Kampf* in 1924

'One must calmly and squarely face the truth that it certainly

cannot have been God's will to give fifty times more land to one nation than another ... If this earth has sufficient room for all, then we ought to have a big enough share to meet all our needs.'

2 Why did Hitler want to expand into the nations of Eastern Europe? *(Outcome 2 – 3 marks)*

(Use the source and recalled knowledge)

3 Look at Source 1.12, taken from Hitler's *Mein Kampf* in 1924. Does this source provide useful evidence of the factors influencing Hitler's foreign policy in the 1930s? *(Outcome 3 – 4 marks)*

QUESTION PRACTICE

4 What were the long term and short term aims of Hitler's foreign policy? *(Outcome 1 – 4 marks)*

5 How useful is Source 1.13 in explaining Hitler's foreign policy in the 1930's? *(Outcome 3 – 4 marks)*

SOURCE 1.13

THE SOURCE.
Die Quelle

QUESTION HINTS

To answer the last question properly means trying to analyse what the cartoon is saying. This means bringing your own knowledge to the source, then asking questions like: What sort of source is it? When from? What point is the caption trying to make? What other information/ideas can you get out of the picture that may help explain it? What aspects of Hitler's foreign policy does it miss out? All this will help you come to a broad conclusion on its view, and therefore answer the question on how helpful it is in explaining Hitler's foreign policy.

Another sort of Intermediate 2 question is the comparison. (The following example uses the same cartoon of Hitler as in Source 1.13)

QUESTION PRACTICE

6 In which way does the cartoon in Source 1.13 agree with the claim made by the historian William Carr in the following source? *(Outcome 3 – 4 marks)*

SOURCE 1.14

'... the need to win and keep mass support during his rise to power in the early 1930s influenced the foreign policy Hitler preached in public. Attacks on the Treaty of Versailles plus appeals for all German speaking people to be joined into one

state, never failed to arouse enthusiasm in audiences which were used to the idea that Germany had been treated shabbily in 1919.'

There is also the possibility of an 8-mark short essay.

What were the main reasons for Germany's aggressive foreign policy in the 1930s? *(Outcomes 1 and 2 – 8 marks)*

NAZI GERMANY 1933–1935: PREPARING THE GROUND

HITLER COMES TO POWER

When Hitler came to power in January 1933, we see that he had some definite foreign policy aims in mind; first of all, he would try to fulfil the election promises he had made to the German people about further revision of the terms of Versailles. So, while it is highly unlikely that Hitler was immediately planning a major war, he was convinced that Nazism was going to be a 'Thousand Year Reich' and he would have to 'prepare the ground' for this.

Since during Hitler's first couple of years in power his major priorities would have been domestic matters, it was therefore a time when he could 'play himself in' as far as foreign affairs were concerned. He would try to get himself established, keep his foreign policy relatively low-key and unaggressive and look to cause no great disturbances on the international scene. He was able to continue the revisionist work of the earlier Weimar government, and in some ways, cash in on their preparations by making gains from where they had done the hard work.

Hitler did at least want to prepare his army generals for the future, by giving a broad picture of the plans he had in mind. In February 1933 he therefore gave a *Speech to his generals* in which he laid out his thinking and put his own personal stamp on policy matters.

SOURCE 2.1 Speech to the German generals

2. Foreign policy. Keep up the battle against Versailles. **Get equality of rights in Geneva Conference. Try to get allies**.
4. Building up the armed forces. Most important thing for achieving goal of regaining political power. **National service must be reintroduced**.
How should political power be used when it has been gained? Perhaps fighting for new export possibilities – and probably better – conquering new living space in the east and ruthlessly bringing it under German control.

It may be that this speech was a bit of *propaganda* , just to impress the generals, but we do see that although Hitler ended up talking about his long-term aims, he also covered his three short-term aims (the three statements in bold in the source.)

WHAT DO YOU THINK?

❶ How far are Hitler's objectives in his *Speech to his generals*, similar to his policies in the 1920 Nazi Party Programme?

❷ How valuable is Hitler's *Speech to his generals* as evidence of Hitler's foreign policy?

As expected, the main issues that Hitler raised in his *Speech to his generals*, all came under the heading of Revising Versailles, so let us look at these one by one.

LEAVING THE DISARMAMENT CONFERENCE AT GENEVA (OCTOBER 1933)

The *League of Nations* had organised the Geneva Disarmament Conference which had started in 1932, and was therefore already in session when Hitler came to power. Britain believed that letting Germany re-arm at a controlled rate was the best policy, while France did not want to give anything away to Germany at all. By 1933, a rough deal had been drawn up to let Germany re-arm at a certain rate, to reach equality in five years. France put conditions on this re-armament, meaning that Germany was only to reach equality in eight years. This looked like the best deal that Germany would be offered and they were on the brink of accepting it. After all, it was better than nothing, since it would let Germany have an army of 200 000 men which would be double the size laid down at Versailles.

Hitler was having none of this. He doubted if Britain, France or the League had the power or nerve to force Germany to accept anything, so he told the Conference that he wasn't accepting their restrictions on Germany's freedom to re-arm. On 14th October 1933 he announced that Germany was withdrawing from the Conference and then left the League of Nations as well. Hitler made his leaving a virtue. In his leaving speech he blamed the other states for their unjust treatment of Germany. He said:

SOURCE 2.2

'*By the deliberate refusal to give us real moral and material equality, the German nation and its Governments have been profoundly humiliated.*'

SOURCE 2.3 *Hitler shortly after leaving the Disarmament Conference of the League of Nations, October 1933*

Source 2.4 sums up quite well the problem facing the allied statesmen when faced with Hitler's demands. An armed Hitler is sitting on a tied-up Peace, claiming he wants the disarmament clauses in the Versailles Treaty to be followed by everyone. The allied statesmen have no answer to this; Hitler seems more peace-loving than them.

Hitler's generals had feared to return to Germany empty-handed, but Hitler showed a better sense of feeling for the mood of the German people. He returned from Geneva with nothing but made out he had achieved a great triumph. He then held a *plebiscite* to ask the German people what they thought of his policies. Around 95% said he had done the right thing. We shall see several occasions where Hitler had an intuitive feeling for what was right at the time, and where he overcame reason and sense with his 'fingertip feeling' for what he could get away with.

WHAT DO YOU THINK?

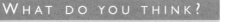

What was the difference between the attitude of the Weimar government towards making a deal at the Disarmament Conference, and Hitler's attitude?

"WELL – WHAT ARE YOU GOING TO DO ABOUT IT NOW?"

SOURCE 2.4 *Cartoon by Low, from the Evening Standard*

GAINING ALLIES: THE GERMAN PACT WITH POLAND (JANUARY 1934)

Hitler never wanted to be in the League of Nations anyway. Nazism, as its title suggests, was a *national* philosophy, not an international one. Hitler didn't want to be tied into international deals and agreements, he wanted the flexibility to be able to make and break deals with any nation as it suited him. This would let him exploit any situation as it arose. He would be prepared to use any nation that could give him an edge. Clearly France was the major obstacle to Germany's progress, but Hitler couldn't tackle France head on, he would have to be more indirect. Hitler felt that it would benefit Germany if France could be separated from some of her friends; he therefore offered Poland and Czechoslovakia 10 year *non-aggression pacts* with Germany. Both of these nations had been newly created in 1919 and both had deals with France to protect their security. There was no really good reason why either should see a deal with Germany (the *loser* in the last war) as a better bet than keeping its deal with France. Czechoslovakia said it wasn't interested in a deal, but Poland responded. Poland possibly considered Russia to be a greater threat to its own security than Germany. If that were true then knowing where they stood with Germany over Russia might be more use to Poland than having French help over Germany. By January 1934 a non-aggression pact was worked out between Germany and Poland. In military terms, this pact was quite meaningless, but it took Poland away from its friendship with France.

WHAT DO YOU THINK?

One historian called the German deal with Poland '*a considerable success*' for Hitler. Why did he think this? (Answer this question by seeing a success as a gain compared with what it has cost).

RE-ARMAMENT PROGRAMME (DECEMBER 1933 . . . THROUGH TO MARCH–JUNE 1935)

Having left the Disarmament Conference, Hitler considered his options for the size and pace of the build up of his armed forces. His generals put forward a plan in December 1933 for the development of a German army (known as the *Reichswehr*), of 21 divisions by 1937 and the introduction of a one year short-service *conscription* . This would have to be in secret since it was against the terms of Versailles, but the result would be an army of 300 000 men. Hitler told his generals that he wanted this number by April 1935.

In secret, Germany was also building up its airforce (known as the *Luftwaffe*), and by the end of 1934 this had reached 2000 planes. Much of this arms build-up was an open secret but Hitler was waiting for the right moment to publicly announce that he had *repudiated* yet another term of the Treaty of Versailles. That moment came in March 1935, when Britain and France were distracted by Italy and the Abyssinian Crisis.

On 9th March 1935, in an interview to the *Daily Mail,* the existence of the *Luftwaffe* was formally admitted. Then, on 16th March 1935 Hitler announced that Germany was introducing conscription and would build up an army of 36 divisions to a total of 550 000 men. This would in fact make it larger than France's. Hitler said,

SOURCE 2.5

'*... The German government considers it impossible to stand back any longer from taking the necessary measures to protect the German Reich, or even* *hide the knowledge of our re-armament from other nations. It does not intend in re-arming Germany to create an instrument for war-like purposes, but on the contrary, it will be exclusively for defence and for keeping the peace.'*

Britain and France were horrified at this major breach of the terms of Versailles but could do nothing. They held a meeting with Italy (at Stresa) where they declared their solemn disapproval of Hitler's plans and promised to work together. This was all quite meaningless since, at that moment, Britain and France were considering how they could stop Mussolini's own plans to invade Abyssinia, so Mussolini was hardly likely to consider joining them in a war against Germany!

In fact, Britain, in keeping with its view that Germany should be permitted to re-arm at a controlled rate, was already feeling that France's stubborn views on keeping Germany disarmed, were a greater obstacle to European peace. Therefore, totally out of self-interest and without consulting France, Britain set about collaborating with Germany in removing the last military term of Versailles!

On 18th June 1935 Britain and Germany signed the **Anglo-German Naval deal**. Britain agreed to let Germany have ' *parity in the air* ' and also build up its naval forces to a level that was 35% of Britain's. Germany was also to be allowed an *equal* number of submarines. Considering that Germany's 1935 naval strength was almost nil, what Britain was in fact doing was giving Germany the go-ahead for a major naval build up. Britain agreed to 'parity in the air' because it was felt that there was nothing Britain could do to stop Germany getting this anyway.

Winston Churchill spoke up against Britain's policy of letting Germany re-arm. He said:

SOURCE 2.6

'There is no mistaking what Germany is doing. At the end of the Great War we said that there must be no more war, yet Germany is now moving along the path of war again. What will this new army be used for? Are submarines and bombers to be used for defence? Hitler must be made to stop his aggressive actions.'

However, most people in Britain saw the Anglo-German naval deal as a sign that Hitler wanted closer ties with Britain and that it would now be possible to negotiate over other problem areas. France however just felt betrayed.

As the historian A. Adamthwaite noted:

SOURCE 2.7

'Britain's attitude was realistic. She felt that Germany was going to increase her naval strength whatever happened and that an agreement was necessary to keep this increase as low as possible. France resented Britain's ready acceptance of Germany breaking the terms of Versailles.'

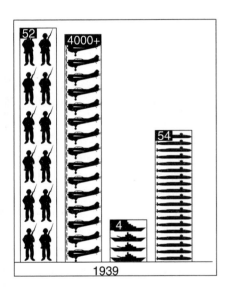

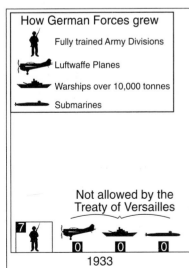

SOURCE 2.8 *How the German Armed Forces grew*

The consequence of Germany breaking free from the armament restrictions of Versailles, was that she could now build up her weapons as she pleased, and there was little that Britain and France could now do to stop it.

By the middle of 1935 therefore, Hitler had done a fair bit of 'ground clearing'. He had established himself in power and had tackled diplomatic issues with confidence.

Two other events in 1934–35 show his assured style . . .

♦ **Austria.** In July 1934 Austrian Nazis murdered the Austrian Chancellor Dollfuss. They rose up in rebellion, expecting German help. This did not please the Italian leader Mussolini, who saw himself as Austria's protector. He sent four divisions of Italian troops to the Brenner Pass and threatened to invade Austria and impose his own control, even if that meant kicking the Germans out. Hitler could see that things were going too fast, he liked to be in control of events but this was out of his hands. He realised the timing was all wrong and he could see that his 'enemies' were united against him. He backed down, declared his peaceful intentions towards Austria, *purged* the Austrian Nazi party and then did what he was best at; let the situation tick over until he was ready to intervene when *he* thought the time was right. The attempted take-over of Austria in July 1934 could have been a disaster for Hitler. He had only been in power for 18 months and inexperience could have pushed him towards taking inadvisable action. That sense he had of the 'rightness of the time' however, showed itself in Hitler's handling of this incident.

♦ **Saar.** The Treaty of Versailles permitted France to occupy the German province of Saarland, as a guarantee that reparation payments would be paid. The agreement was that after 15 years, a plebiscite would be held to ask the population of Saar what they wanted to happen to their state.

The time was up in January 1935 and, without any problems, the plebiscite was held, giving a not-unexpected 90% vote for return to Germany. It can be seen that, in a sense, this success was nothing whatsoever to do with Hitler, it was just the natural working out of an agreement made 15 years earlier. However, the Nazi propaganda machine went into over-drive, boasting this as a triumphant achievement of Nazi foreign policy. Hitler had the confidence to be able to portray it as something that *he* had worked at and a success for his policy of Versailles revisionism. It was really no big deal but it was another example of the way Hitler didn't miss a chance of presenting a situation in the best light for himself.

WHAT DO YOU THINK?

1 Some historians have claimed that the reason for Hitler's success was his ability to pick his moment when he could see that his enemies were divided. Does the evidence support this view of Hitler and his rearmament programme?

2 What arguments can be put for and against Britain making the naval deal with Germany in 1935?

SOURCE 2.9 *Hitler in Saarbrucken*

WHAT DO YOU THINK?

The first two years in power are often the time of greatest danger for any national leader, due to their inexperience in the ways of international diplomacy. Do you agree that *'Hitler was more successful than he maybe could have expected'* up to the end of 1935?

QUESTION PRACTICE

(See pages 93–99 for advice on different types of questions)

SOURCE 2.10 Conflict and Co-operation: Doran and Dargie

'In 1934, Hitler secretly began to build up his armed forces. A year later he openly introduced conscription for all German men.'

1 In which ways did Germany build up its armed forces after Hitler came to power?

(Outcome 1 – 3 marks)
(Use the source and recall)

QUESTION PRACTICE

SOURCE 2.11 Sir Anthony Eden MP in 1935

Who are we to complain? We have failed to disarm. France refuses to disarm despite promises made sixteen years ago. Are we really going to bully Germany again? Let Germany rearm and give her people work.

2 Why did Britain and France let Germany rearm?

(Outcome 2 – 4 marks)
(Use the source and recall)

3 Describe how Germany rearmed between 1933 and 1935

(Outcome 2 – 4 marks)

HITLER'S FIRST BIG STEP: THE RHINELAND 1936

This chapter will do four main things:

- explain the background to Hitler's policy over the demilitarised zone of the Rhineland
- describe the circumstances of the re-occupation of the demilitarised zone
- discuss the French and British reaction to the re-occupation of this zone
- weigh up the effects of Germany's action in re-militarising the zone

SOURCE 3.1 *Map of Rhineland Area*

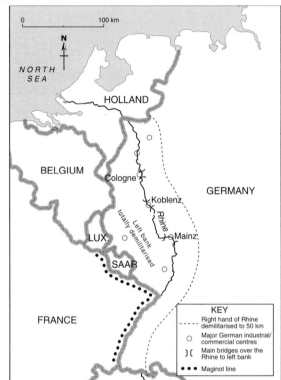

SOURCE 3.2 Terms of Treaty of Versailles 1919 concerning the Rhineland

Article 42. *Germany is forbidden to build or keep any foritifcations either on the left bank of the Rhine or on the right bank to the west of a line drawn fifty kilometres to the east of the Rhine.*

Article 43. *In the area defined above, it is also forbidden to keep or assemble armed forces, either permanently or temporarily, hold military manoeuvres of any kind, as well as the upkeep of all permanent works of mobilisation.*

Article 44. *If Germany breaks the provisions of Articles 42 and 43 in any way, she shall be regarded as committing a hostile act against the powers which signed this treaty.*

THE BACKGROUND TO HITLER'S POLICY ON THE RHINELAND

One of the key areas of Hitler's foreign policy was to try to dismantle the terms of the Treaty of Versailles. His first three years in power show that Hitler made steady gains in his revision of the Treaty. There were several reasons why this policy had been such a good one to follow.

◆ It was almost a 'no-risk' policy for Hitler since there was nothing new or unusual about it. Most of the foreign ministers of Weimar Germany up until 1933 had also followed this policy and had made gradual gains in revising the harshness of the terms of Versailles.

◆ German opposition to and 'chipping away at' Versailles was actually what the Allies expected Germany to do. Generally, British foreign policy had been to consent to Germany doing this and try to give way to German *revisionist* demands at a controlled rate. (We saw that at the 1932–33 Geneva Disarmament Conference, Britain's policy was *not* to resist Germany's plans for re-armament but rather to attempt to regulate it by letting Germany re-arm gradually).

◆ A policy of revision of Versailles was always well accepted inside Germany. There was a deep and lasting feeling of resentment in most German people, of the terms imposed upon Germany at Versailles.

WHAT DO YOU THINK?

Why had Germany been able to revise the terms of the Treaty before 1935?

By 1936, it seemed as if there only were three or four major terms of Versailles which Germany would have wanted to revise. However, these were all *territorial* matters on which the British and French governments might not be so ready to budge. They might not be ready to stand back and let Germany continue its revisionist policy if it now became a matter of giving back land.

By 1936 therefore, Hitler was at a crossroads. If he wanted to continue a policy which was popular with Germans, then he needed to keep on revising Versailles. However, this now became a riskier business since the stakes were higher because he wanted to take over territory. The old wartime allies, Britain and France, still had greater military power than Germany, even though Germany had re-introduced conscription in March 1935. Hitler risked losing everything if he pushed them into a war, which Germany was not yet strong enough to fight.

An interesting question here is why Hitler didn't just turn to some other aspects of his foreign policy and develop those areas instead. The answer of course is that revision of Versailles was fundamental to Hitler's foreign policy and *all* other aspects came afterwards. In other words, Hitler could not pursue his racial or *Lebensraum* policies until he had got Versailles (especially the demilitarised Rhineland) out of the way. It could be argued that, in practice, Hitler did not have a choice about what foreign policy to follow since revision of Versailles was only one that he could pursue. The only thing in Hitler's control was the timing of this policy.

Why then was it so important for Hitler to deal with this problem of the demilitarisation of the Rhineland?

Amongst the 440 articles (or terms) which made up the Treaty of Versailles, three of them referred to the demilitarisation of the Rhineland. These were Articles 42, 43 and 44. These terms had been

WHAT DO YOU THINK?

If Hitler wanted to continue revising the terms of Versailles *after* 1933, why did he face new problems compared to those that had faced German leaders before 1933?

put in because, although France had been victorious in the First World War, she still felt very insecure about the future. Her neighbour, the defeated Germany, was still so much stronger and bigger than France was. German industrial wealth was four times that of France, and Germany's population was 50% larger. The problem, as France's Marshall Foch said (with reference to Germany's population of 60 million and France's 40 million) *'How do you make one Frenchman equal one and a half Germans?'*

The question troubling the French statesmen was how to bring down Germany's advantage so that she would not want to start another war. Part of the answer lay in reparations and disarmament, but a key idea was to entirely demilitarise the left bank of the Rhine and also the right bank to a depth of 50 kilometres (see Source 3.1). This demilitarisation placed great limits on Germany's western defences. She could not put any weapons, soldiers or military installations into the large Rhineland area, and, up until 1929, there had been an allied commission (and military forces) there to make sure these regulations were kept.

These restrictions on Germany should have helped make France feel more secure. After all Germany could never really start a war on France now because her western border area was undefended, giving France an open route into Germany's industrial heartland. Germany would therefore be deterred from starting a war to the west. Also, Germany could not get too aggressive with any of her eastern neighbours (who might be friends with France), since France could always come to their aid with a military advance through the undefended Rhineland. Germany would therefore be deterred from starting a war to the east.

An added security here was that these terms that had been *imposed on* Germany in 1919 had also been *agreed to* by Germany in 1925. France had been worried that Germany might try to evade the terms of Versailles by claiming that she had no choice in signing them. However, in 1925 the European Great Powers had met again at Locarno and in an atmosphere of peace and *rapprochement*, the German delegates had freely entered into a promise to never again try to change Germany's western borders (with France or Belgium), by *'flagrant aggression'* (in other words, by warlike methods). France, Germany, UK and Italy had all signed the Locarno agreement. This had helped to re-assure France and, taken with all the other restrictions still placed on Germany, should have been enough to make France feel secure.

However, in 1935 France began to make approaches towards a friendship with Soviet Russia. France considered that this would help build up her connections in Eastern Europe, so she started negotiations with Soviet Russia about having a mutual assistance pact between the two countries.

It was now that a fatal flaw of the Locarno agreement of 1925 showed itself. France had indeed obtained a guarantee from Germany in 1925 that Germany would never try to alter its western borders by force, but the 'price' of this was an understanding

WHAT DO YOU THINK?

1. Why did France feel insecure against Germany after the end of the First World War?
2. Why would the terms of Versailles help France feel secure?
3. Why would the terms of Locarno help France feel even more secure?

between France and Germany at Locarno that Germany's *eastern* borders were her own business. It was largely up to Germany what she did there; that would not be a worry to the French.

Germany, in late 1935, very quickly realised that if France continued her negotiations with Russia, she was breaking her side of the bargain at Locarno, which was to leave Eastern Europe alone. The obvious argument, in Hitler's mind, was that if France could break the terms of Locarno, then so could Germany, and the way that Germany could break it would be to re-militarise the Rhineland zone.

The French government had realised that Germany might see their treaty with Russia in this way, and also realised that Germany might see it as 'encirclement'. Neither the French government nor the British government however, had drawn up any plans on what to do in the event of Germany trying to take advantage of the situation.

Hitler, meantime, had the situation under close review. This note by von Hassel, the German ambassador in Italy, on 14th February 1936 sums up Hitler's thinking:

SOURCE 3.3

'The question was whether Germany should take the signing of the French pact with Russia as grounds for denouncing Locarno and once more stationing troops in the demilitarised zone. The latter, seen from the military point of view, was an absolute necessity. ... Until now he had always thought that the spring of 1937 would be the right moment. Political developments made one wonder whether the psychological moment had not arrived now.'

This revealing note suggests that just about everybody knew about the chances of a German military move into the Rhineland. Even the British ambassador in Berlin, Sir Eric Phipps, had written in December 1935:

SOURCE 3.4

'I fear the Zone will be re-occupied whenever a favourable excuse presents itself.'

Von Hassell's note also reveals the importance of choosing the right moment to try to 'get away' with an action. We have noted already that the ability to 'pick the right moment' was something where Hitler showed himself to be particularly talented.

QUESTION PRACTICE

(See pages 93–99 for advice on different types of questions)

1 How useful is a source like Von Hassell's note, Source 3.3, in helping to understand German foreign policy in 1936?

(Outcome 3 – 4 marks)

2 Describe the events which led up to the Rhineland Crisis.

(Outcome 2 – 4 marks)

To earn the 4 marks in question 2, you should write a few lines each on:

a describing the military situation in the Rhineland from 1919

b describing what Germany thought about it and what it might plan to do

c saying what France did in 1935–36 that turned the situation into a crisis

THE CIRCUMSTANCES OF THE MILITARY RE-OCCUPATION OF THE RHINELAND

By the end of February 1936, Hitler had made his mind up that there was a golden opportunity for Germany to take action over the Rhineland. It was the situation in France that had led him to this conclusion.

The French parliament was going to *ratify* the Franco-Russian Agreement on 27th February 1936. The French politicians were divided over whether it was actually a good idea, and being divided among themselves helped Hitler. He therefore made his mind up on 1st March to send German troops into the Rhineland, breaking the terms of the Treaty of Versailles and the Locarno Pact.

This military re-occupation was to take place on Saturday 7th March. The German generals were very reluctant to make the plans or put them into operation. They were '*horrified*' because their forces were so weak compared to those of France. Hitler however, appreciated more than they did, that victories can be won when the time is ripe, not just when your forces are strongest. You just need to pick the right moment.

To re-assure them, Hitler said that if there was any opposition, the German troops would withdraw.

WHAT DO YOU THINK?

1. Why did Hitler think it was a golden opportunity to re-militarise the Rhineland in early March 1936?
2. Why did Hitler face opposition inside Germany, to his plans to re-militarise the Rhineland and how did he overcome this opposition?

SOURCE 3.5 *Crowds cheer German soldiers on the march over the Hohenzollern Bridge in Cologne, entering the demilitarised left bank of the Rhineland*

At dawn on Saturday 7th March 1936, just over 20 000 fully armed German troops marched into the demilitarised right bank of the Rhineland, and, more famously, over the Rhine bridges into the demilitarised left bank.

Hitler chose a Saturday because the British and French governments would not be in a good position to react over the weekend. Their parliaments would not be sitting again until Monday, by which time two day's worth of newspapers would have been produced for the public to read, in which Hitler could make some fine sounding declarations of peace which would present his actions in a better light.

Hitler accompanied his warlike move with some attractive promises. He offered:

◆ a non-aggression pact with everyone for 25 years
◆ a new equal de-militarised zone for the French!
◆ to rejoin the League of Nations if the Treaty of Versailles was separated from it

By Monday, it was *these* promises that were in the newspapers and on peoples' minds, not the fact that the Rhineland was now re-militarised.

A careful consideration of each of Hitler's three promises shows that they were ridiculous. He was promising to keep a deal for 25 years when the evidence so far was that he couldn't keep one for even three years. Then an equal French de-militarisation of their side of the Rhine would require the dismantling of the entire *Maginot Line* and the loss of billions of French francs. Lastly, Versailles could not be disconnected from the League of Nations since the creation of the League was a part of the Versailles terms.

Hitler's promises were just a smokescreen to distract attention from what he had done.

Hitler knew he had taken a big chance. He said:

SOURCE 3.6

'The 48 hours after the march into the Rhineland were the most nerve-wracking of my life.... If the French had then marched into the Rhineland, we would have had to withdraw with our tails between our legs, for the military resources at our disposal would have been wholly inadequate for even a moderate resistance.'

Hitler need not have worried. There was no military opposition to his action, even though, as he is later reported to have said to Albert Speer (his wartime Minister of Armaments):

SOURCE 3.7

'We had no army worth mentioning.... If the French had taken any action, we would have been easily defeated; our resistance would have been over in a couple of days.'

Hitler's ability to pick the right moment had been proved yet again: another major term of Versailles had been revised in Germany's favour. The historian C.L. Mowat summed it up by saying:

SOURCE 3.8

'Hitler had got safely away with his swag.'

WHAT DO YOU THINK?

1 Explain the two ways that Hitler behaved quite cleverly in his planning for sending the German troops into the Rhineland? (The words 'weekend' and 'smokescreen' should help you with this answer).

2 Look at the historian C.L. Mowat's view of Hitler's action (Source 3.8). Can you describe in your own words what you think his view is?

QUESTION PRACTICE   *i2*

Study Hitler's words starting with *'The 48 hours after the march....'* (Source 3.6)

1 Explain why Hitler's actions were risky.

(Use the source and recall)

(Outcome 2 – 4 marks)

2 How useful is this source in helping understand German foreign policy in March 1936?

(Outcome 3 – 4 marks)

3 How well does Source 3.9 explain the events of the Rhineland in 1936?

(4 marks)

(Outcome 3 – 4 marks)

(Use the source and recall)

QUESTION HINTS

SOURCE 3.9 *Goose cartoon by Shepard from* Punch

THE GOOSE-STEP.
"GOOSEY GOOSEY GANDER,
WHITHER DOST THOU WANDER?"
"ONLY THROUGH THE RHINELAND.—
PRAY EXCUSE MY BLUNDER!"

A cartoon like this can be a very useful way of considering points of view *from the time*, on Hitler's action in re-militarising the Rhineland. You should be able to study it, and pick out particular parts of the cartoon that are trying to make a point. You should then be able to compare these with your own knowledge and come to a conclusion about the importance or accuracy of the points being made.

Ask yourself what the following points are supposed to mean:
- the goose/what is in its beak/the words on the tag
- the weapons/helmet over the eyes
- the torn piece of paper on the ground
- the title and words of the caption below
- the flags in the windows

All these points give you clues about what the cartoonist thinks. Do these points make you think the cartoonist is for or against the German action?

WHY DID THE FRENCH AND BRITISH REACT THE WAY THEY DID TO THE GERMAN MILITARY RE-OCCUPATION OF THE RHINELAND?

THE FRENCH RESPONSE

There were several factors which influenced the way that the French government reacted to the German move into the Rhineland.
- *The political situation inside France.* The government in France was a temporary and divided government, waiting for elections to be held. This government was not sure that there was support inside France for taking firm action against Germany if that led to a general war. The French *right wing* opposed the deal with Russia anyway, while the *left wing* seemed more prepared to swallow Hitler's promises of peace for the future. The weak French government felt that its best plan was to do nothing.
- *France's relationship with Britain.* France may have been more prepared to do something if it could have been sure of getting support from its old war-time ally Britain. Unfortunately, France did not know where it now stood with Britain. The Anglo-German Naval Agreement of June 1935 (see page 19) had convinced the French that Britain was unreliable as an ally.
- *The Military situation inside France.* France had always been worried about Germany's military strength. Since 1930 France had invested billions of francs in constructing a heavily fortified line of defences along the French side of the border with Germany. This was called the *Maginot Line* and it had given France at least some sense of security against its powerful neighbour. The effect of having the Maginot Line was to make

SOURCE 3.10 *The Maginot line. It is easy to see why the French generals believed it was so strong, and therefore made them defence-minded.*

the French generals and government very defensive minded. They felt safe behind the line and were reluctant to come out from behind it. This became known as the 'Maginot mentality'. The view of the French generals was that if the French army was ordered to go into the Rhineland to throw out the Germans, that was a risk, but if they stayed behind the Maginot line that was safe. They therefore advised the French government to stay behind the line.

♦ *The French were too ready to believe the worst.* The French government fooled itself about what was really happening and believed the worst. It was true that Germany had re-introduced conscription and started re-building an air force in 1935, but their total military forces were still vastly inferior to those of France by March 1936. Germany had sent only three battalions of troops into the Rhineland, but French intelligence sources greatly over-estimated the size of the German military forces. The historian A.J.P. Taylor commented that:

SOURCE 3.11

'General Gamelin believed that Germany had one million men under arms of which 300 000 were already in the Rhineland.'

Skilful German propaganda may have helped to make the French army believe this figure and it was enough to make the French government pause and wonder if it really wanted a fight with such a force. It is difficult to know how they managed to convince themselves it was such a large invading force when the *Yorkshire Post*, in its headline of Monday 9th March, stated more accurately that *'10,000 German soldiers march into the Rhineland'*

This spider diagram in Source 3.12 will help to explain the factors that influenced France in her decision not to take action against Germany.

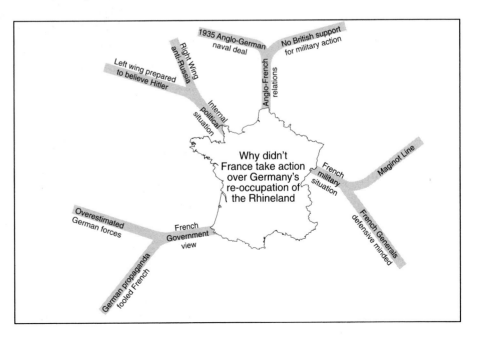

THE BRITISH RESPONSE

Just as with France, there were several factors which influenced the way that the British government reacted to the German move into the Rhineland.

◆ *Sympathy with Germany*. There was considerable sympathy inside Britain for the German point of view over the Rhineland. From quite early in the 1920s, the mood inside Britain had swung towards thinking that The Treaty of Versailles had been an injustice imposed upon Germany, and that the terms of Versailles needed to be changed. Many thought Germany's behaviour over the Rhineland was therefore quite understandable and Britain should not stand in their way in taking back what rightfully belonged to them. This view is summed up at the time by Lord Lothian's comment that:

SOURCE 3.13

'They are only going into their own back garden.'

◆ *Britain's relationship with France*. There may have been more support inside Britain for taking action if Britain's relations with France had been better. In addition to the general feeling that a lot of the problems with Germany were actually *caused* by French stubbornness over Germany, there was also the fact that in 1936, the two old allies were not on as good terms as they could have been. The Anglo-German Naval Agreement of 1935 had soured relations since Britain had not consulted France about it in advance. When the French Foreign Secretary came to London, looking for advice and support, he received a cool reaction from the British government to the idea of strong opposition to Germany.

◆ *France's relations with Russia*. The way the French government were behaving with regard to Russia also influenced British relations with France. The French wanted the mutual assistance pact with Soviet Russia to boost their sense of security but the British government and many of the British people had a great suspicion of France for wanting to make a deal with Communist Russia. Many felt that a strong Germany was needed to stop the spread of communist ideas into Western Europe. This view is summed up by a British diplomat, Harold Nicholson, who asked himself what would be the result of Britain and France acting together to remove Germany from the Rhineland:

SOURCE 3.14

'Naturally we shall win and enter Berlin, but what is the good of that? It would only mean communism in Germany and France and that is why the Russians are so keen on it.'

◆ *The Military view inside Britain*. The British government consulted with its own military experts about the sort of military intervention Britain might make. The advisory group of senior members of the three armed forces (it was called CIGS which was short for Chiefs of the Imperial General Staff) was usually very cautious about British prospects of military victory, and told the government so. This was of course, what the British government generally wanted to hear because it justified the fact that they planned to do nothing. On 12th March 1936, CIGS sent a memo to the government which included comments like:

SOURCE 3.15

'... any question of a war with Germany ... would be thoroughly dangerous ... if there is the smallest danger of being drawn into commitments which might lead to a war with Germany.'

This pessimistic view of Britain's chances of winning any fight with Germany led the British government to decide that it should not commit itself to any firm action to support France.

We can see therefore that there were a range of different reasons inside Britain which made the British refuse to help the French to use military force against Germany in the Rhineland. The government was not stupid, it did realise that Germany's action was a threat, the question was how to respond to it. The answer at that time was considered to be one of *appeasement*, bargaining with Hitler, hoping his promises of peace were true and that his ambitions could be satisfied without needing to go to war.

QUESTION PRACTICE   *i*1

SOURCE 3.16 From the historian R.A.C. Parker in his book *Chamberlain and Appeasement*:

'Two facts influenced the course of the Rhineland Crisis. One was the French decision to only take action if they had British support, the other, was the entirely predictable decision by the British to do nothing that might upset the previously improving relations with Germany.'

1 What was the attitude of the British people towards the Rhineland crisis?   (Outcome 1 – 3 marks)
(Use the source and recall)

WHAT WERE THE EFFECTS OF GERMANY'S ACTION IN RE-MILITARISING THE ZONE?

It is easy for historians to look back at March 1936 and see it as a turning point. It was not so easy at the time to see it that way. The historian W. Carr described Germany's action as:

SOURCE 3.17

'... a real turning point in the inter-war years which marked the beginning of the shift in the balance of power away from Paris and back to Berlin.'

However, it is hard to find evidence from the British newspapers, the public or government members, that anyone *at that time* saw it in those significant terms.

Harold Macmillan, who was a junior MP at that time, came closest to prophesy when he said on 20th March 1936:

SOURCE 3.18

'There will be no war now. But unless a settlement is made... there will be war in 1940.'

He at least saw the significance of the event *at that time*.

THE EFFECTS OF THE RE-MILITARISATION OF THE RHINELAND ON BRITAIN AND FRANCE

◆ It denied France the security of the '*buffer zone*' with Germany that she had previously had. (In French eyes this made the Maginot Line even more important for French security.)

◆ France's ability to help any of its allies in Eastern Europe (like Czechoslovakia) was now severely undermined. Since Hitler very quickly fortified the German side of the border with France, there was now no chance of France making any serious attack on Germany. This meant Germany could do as she liked on her eastern borders, *against France's allies*, without France being able to offer any help. In this way it can be seen that the re-militarisation of the Rhineland did indeed alter the balance of power in Europe since it made France far less effective as a major power.

◆ France lost a lot of credibility. The general view was that she had some justification to fight to remove German forces from the Rhineland and guarantee the keeping of the terms of Versailles. If she was not prepared to fight in March 1936 over a justified grievance, what were the chances of being able to depend on her to fight on some other occasion?

◆ Plenty of observers inside Britain realised that Britain had suffered a setback in their international position. Anthony Eden, the British Foreign Secretary at the time, realised Britain was being taken in by Germany and said that what was needed was to:

SOURCE 3.19

'... try and correct public opinion which was assuming that Germany was the "white sheep" whereas really she was the "black sheep"'

This shows that Eden at least, recognised that the British public had not understood the true extent of the loss that Britain had suffered, and that they had fallen for Hitler's lies. Eden also was well aware that by re-militarising the Rhineland, it made it easier for Germany to invade France through Belgium, as they had in 1914. In the event, the German invasion of France in 1940, took place just to the north of the end of the Maginot Line, through the Ardennes, in Southern Belgium. This would have been impossible if the Germans had not been able to re-militarise the Rhineland in 1936. This is why, as we said at the start of this chapter, that re-militarising the Rhineland was absolutely crucial to Hitler's whole military and diplomatic strategy in Europe. Without it, nothing else could have happened. Eden neatly summed up the effect of the re-militarisation (and his opinion of the French!) by saying:

SOURCE 3.20

'Britain's frontier with Germany is now the English Channel'

◆ There is evidence that some leading political figures inside Britain, now knew more of the nature of the man they were up against, and knew not to trust him. This view seems at odds however, with the fact that in 1936–38 the British government followed a policy of appeasement where it constantly showed Hitler that it *did* believe what he was saying.

Anthony Eden however, in a realistic report to the Cabinet, said that:

SOURCE 3.21

'The myth is now exploded that Hitler only repudiates treaties by force. We must be prepared for him to repudiate any treaty even if freely negotiated when it becomes inconvenient, and when Germany is sufficiently strong and the circumstances are otherwise favourable for doing so.'

Sir Austen Chamberlain also said in the Rhineland debate in the House of Commons on 26th March 1936:

SOURCE 3.22

'We have got to recognise that German standards of conduct are not ours, that German ethics are not ours …'

WHAT DO YOU THINK?

❶ In which ways do Anthony Eden and Austen Chamberlain agree?

❷ How useful is a source like Anthony Eden's report, in helping us to understand British foreign policy at that time?

❸ A historian wrote:

SOURCE 3.23

'Most British opinion thought Hitler's move into the Rhineland was regrettable in the way he had done it, but didn't feel particularly threatened by what he had done.'

What evidence is there on these last two pages that:

a The British disapproved of the way that Hitler had remilitarised the Rhineland?

b The British did not feel threatened?

WHAT WERE THE EFFECTS OF THE RE-MILITARISATION OF THE RHINELAND ON GERMANY?

◆ Hitler's status inside Germany was obviously enhanced. He had brought back 'victories' before (e.g. leaving the Geneva Disarmament talks in 1933 and getting back the Saarland in 1935 had both been triumphantly exploited by the Nazis as signs of the new foreign policy success that Germany was having under Hitler). These, however, were nothing compared to the glory of putting German military forces into the Rhineland and getting away with it under the very noses of the French. Hitler was ecstatically received inside Germany when news broke.

◆ Hitler's control over his army generals was now more secure. Many claim that they were the only group that could have removed him at an early stage in his time in power. They had watched and taken orders in 1936, some of them wondering if he would slip up over the Rhineland and if they would have a chance to replace him. By over-riding their caution and forcing them into an action in the Rhineland which they had great doubts about, *and then getting away with it*, Hitler had put all the generals in their place. He had shown that his judgement was better than theirs, the result was that they would now be more hesitant about 'taking him on' and thinking of replacing him.

◆ Germany could now begin to think of making more ambitious plans on their eastern borders. Since France would now find it very difficult to intervene, Hitler could make plans for the revision of more of the territorial terms of Versailles. Austria was a tempting next target.

QUESTION PRACTICE   *i1*

(See pages 93–99 for advice on different types of questions)

SOURCE 3.24 Taken from a Scottish local newspaper, 14th March 1936:

We firmly believe that the great majority of the British people, while admitting Hitler's action in the Rhineland is dangerous, think that it is justifiable. Every effort should be made to see *that stubborn French leaders do not again make a mess of things. The British people do not wish to fight anyone. We are anxious for a settlement that will bring peace to Europe, but we will not get that unless we pay attention to Germany's appeal to be treated fairly.*

1 Is this source useful evidence of the British public's view of the Rhineland crisis?   *(Outcome 3 – 3 marks)*

QUESTION PRACTICE   *i2*

2 Why were the events in the Rhineland in 1936 so important to the future peace of Europe?

(Outcome 2 – 4 marks)

THE TAKE-OVER OF AUSTRIA 1938

INTRODUCTION

Hitler's success in re-militarising the Rhineland in March 1936 had strengthened Germany's position in Europe. It was now less vulnerable to any attack and was in a position to influence diplomatic affairs for itself, rather than just being the 'victim' of what other nations decided. This new confidence is evident in several tactical steps that Germany took.

- July 1936 – Hitler made an **Austro-Germany Agreement** where the two states agreed to consult over foreign policy. It increased Germany's influence over Austria.
- July 1936 – Spanish Civil War started. Germany offered limited but important military support to help the Fascist rebels under General Franco.
- November 1936 – Germany and Italy signed an agreement which became known as the **Rome-Berlin Axis**, where they agreed to share a common foreign policy.

  None of these actions demonstrate that Hitler was making a deliberate plan to prepare for war but they do show that he was confident enough to make diplomatic moves with whoever he liked, as and when he wished.
- In January 1937 Hitler made a speech to the German Reichstag, in which he said *'the time for so called surprises has ended'*, and indeed, 1937 was a quiet year in terms of German diplomacy, with no major event.

The one incident that is worth further investigation is the Hossbach Conference on 5th November 1937. This was a meeting between Hitler, his Foreign and War ministers, and the chiefs of the Army, Navy and Air Force. It is named after Colonel Hossbach who took notes of the meeting. He then wrote up these notes in a document which became known as the Hossbach Memorandum. At the meeting, Hitler gave a review of Germany's future foreign policy aims. He looked at different opportunities for action by Germany that might arise concerning Austria, Czechoslovakia and Poland. He called these 'Cases' and gave them names (Case Otto was Austria, Case Green was Czechoslovakia and Case White was Poland). Because he also said that *'Germany must be ready for war by 1938 and at the latest by 1943–45'*, it looks as if this was Hitler's plan of action for war. The conference therefore seems a significant turning point in German foreign policy, with Hitler now being confident enough to lay down an entire strategy for an aggressive foreign policy (whereas only two years earlier he had been wondering if he could even get away with re-occupying the Rhineland!). However, although it all looks believable because we know that Germany's next foreign policy actions *were* in those three countries, in that order, historians are in great dispute as to whether the Hossbach Memo did add up to a 'grand plan' by Hitler.

Some historians suggest the Conference didn't really take place at all (!) while others saw it as a purely political manoeuvre by Hitler to see which of his military commanders and ministers really supported him. Whether or not you believe the conference was a significant turning point, it was probably still the case that by the end of 1937, Hitler had got a clearer idea of his diplomatic objectives and the European situation in which he was working. He may not have been planning a major war, but he *was* planning to take advantage of opportunities to make Germany greater by further dismantling the terms of the Treaty of Versailles.

WHAT DO YOU THINK?

1. What are the key differences of foreign policy between the 1937 *Hossbach Memo* and Hitler's 1933 *Speech to his generals*?
2. Why do some historians think that the *Hossbach Memo* is a valuable historical document?

SOURCE 4.1 *Map of Austria*

1938 was a year in which Hitler made two big gains. Under his direction and control, Germany was able to take over Austria (this was known as the *Anschluss* or Union) and put Germany in a position to take part of, then all of, Czechoslovakia.

THE ANSCHLUSS

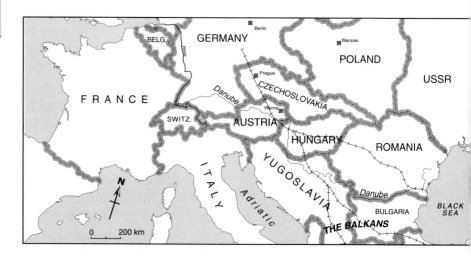

THE BACKGROUND TO HITLER'S POLICY TOWARDS AUSTRIA

Before 1914, Austria-Hungary and Germany were two of the great empires which controlled central Europe. The German Reich (Empire) had been formed almost entirely out of Germans and German speakers. This was in marked contrast to the earlier creation of the Austrian Empire, which had seen a small group of German-speaking Austrians gain control over a vast number of other races, each with their own languages and customs.

The two empires had made a military agreement in the Dual Alliance of 1879. There were many in Germany who saw this as the first step towards them joining together. This would create a 'superstate', a 'Greater German' Empire which would include all German-speakers. People who held this view were known as *Pan-Germans* since they supported the idea of Germans from *all over*, being joined into one state. When the two Empires (usually called the Central Powers) went to war together in 1914, Pan-Germans thought it would lead to the creation of the single great German state that they hoped for. They were to be disappointed.

When the Central Powers were defeated in 1918, the Germans and Austrians were treated in very different ways. Germany was heavily punished at the Versailles settlement, but at the Treaty of St Germain, Austria was spared. She was reduced to a very small state, with her whole empire taken away and new independent states created, but she received no great punishment. She was left largely under the care and supervision of Italy. Article 80 of the Treaty of Versailles was also quite clear in forbidding the joining together of Germany and Austria. There was to be no *Anschluss*, no creation of a 'Greater Germany'. The Pan-German dream seemed to have died.

The dream however, did not entirely disappear. There were plenty of people, like Hitler, who still believed the day would come when all Germans would be united into one state.

In 1924, in *Mein Kampf*, Hitler expressed his thoughts about what should happen:

SOURCE 4.2

'German-Austria must be restored to the great German motherland. And not for economic reasons at all. No, no. Even if the union caused no economic gains, or even if it were to be a disadvantage, it should still take place. People of the same blood ought to be in the same Reich. The German people will have no right to look for colonies overseas until they have brought all their children in Europe together in one state.'

When Hitler came to power in January 1933, Pan Germans must have had great hopes that, under Hitler, their dream of a united German state would soon become a reality.

In fact, inside Austria, some Austrian Nazis were so convinced that an *Anschluss* was about to happen, that in 1934 they attempted to start one by murdering the Austrian Chancellor Dollfuss, believing that Germany would then charge in and take over Austria. (see page 20). Hitler however, realised that the time was not right; he hadn't been in power for long and didn't yet know how the other great powers would react. So Hitler backed off and acted like an *Anschluss* was never really his intention. In fact, he had decided to go for an *evolutionary* approach i.e. wait and see how things turned out. What happened over the next four years rewarded his caution. Italy became involved in other things (Abyssinia and the Spanish Civil War) and Mussolini realised that his days of ordering Hitler about were over. The other great powers seemed to show no interest in sticking up for the tiny independent Austrian state that they had created in 1919. By 1936, Austria was clearly further falling under Germany's influence, rather than Italy's, as shown by the 1936 Austro-German Agreement. (referred to on page 35) It could almost be argued that by 1937 an *Anschluss* was just a matter of time.

We can see therefore that ideas of race and 'German-ness' are given as the chief reasons for Hitler's interest in bringing about the union of Austria and Germany. It may also be the case that the fact that Hitler was Austrian by birth gave him a sense of destiny that his mission was to join the two states. A look at the map in Source 4.1 however, does show that *geographic factors* (control of the Danube river basin, railway access to the Balkans, the surrounding of Czechoslovakia) and *military/economic factors* would offer powerful additional reasons for making an *Anschluss* look so attractive to Hitler

WHAT DO YOU THINK?

1. What did Pan-Germans hope to achieve?
2. What views did Hitler hold that would have pleased Pan-Germans?
3. Why was there no Anschluss in 1934 when the Austrian Nazis first tried it?
4. What would Germany gain by an *Anschluss*?

THE CIRCUMSTANCES OF THE TAKE-OVER OF AUSTRIA IN FEBRUARY–MARCH 1938

After Chancellor Dollfuss was assassinated in 1934, the new Austrian Chancellor was Kurt von Schuschnigg. He faced great problems of social and economic unrest inside Austria and, partly due to the constant agitation, had banned several political parties, including the Nazis. This had not stopped the Austrian Nazis from their campaign of disrupting orderly government through bomb attacks and mass demonstrations. This de-stabilising campaign may or may not have been ordered from Berlin, but it made it hard for Schuschnigg to govern effectively.

SOURCE 4.3 Increasing
pressure *by Low*

INCREASING PRESSURE.

WHAT DO YOU THINK?

Study Source 4.3.

1 What point is this cartoon
   making about:
   a The situation Austria and
   other countries were finding
   themselves in by 1938?
   b The attitude of Britain or
   France (the two standing at
   the left end of the line)?

2 Does the cartoon agree with
   the point above that the
   *Anschluss 'may or may not have
   been ordered from Berlin'*?
   Explain your answer.

Most historians agree that the timing of the Anschluss was not
Hitler's; he took advantage of a situation that arose. By February
1938, Schuschnigg let it be known that he wanted to see Hitler, to
see if the Nazi leader could take steps to control the Nazi party in
Austria. Hitler saw the opportunity to 'push' a little harder over
Austria to see if anything in Germany's favour could come of it. He
therefore summoned Schuschnigg to the Berghof at Berchtesgaden,
Hitler's summer retreat in the German Alps.

There is an important point to make here, that Hitler, of all the
European statesmen, was most happy to operate in an 'off-the-cuff'
situation. He didn't mind disorder and instability, in fact he
encouraged it. He had the maverick attitudes of the unconventional
poker player. While other politicians and statesmen had very
conventional views about their duty to try to create order and peace
out of tricky diplomatic situations, Hitler didn't mind behaving
irrationally and causing disorder. Thus he would shout, bluster,
threaten, have tantrums and behave unexpectedly, often just to see
where it would get him. It was often very much to his advantage.

When Schuschnigg went to Berchtesgaden on February 12th, he
therefore probably did not expect the reaction he received. He went
there as the 'injured party' wanting to complain about things.
Instead, he was treated to a display of temper and verbal aggression
and threats by Hitler that was really entirely out of order at a
meeting of two national leaders. Hitler raged at him that:

SOURCE 4.4

*'The whole history of Austria is just one long act of high treason. That was so in
the past and it is the same today. This historical nonsense must come to an end,*

and I can tell you here and now that I am absolutely determined to finish this. The German Reich is one of the Great Powers and nobody will raise his voice if it settles its border problems.

I have only to give an order and in one single night all your ridiculous defences will be blown to bits. You don't seriously believe that you can stop me, or even delay me for half an hour, do you?

Think it over, Herr Schuschnigg, think it over well. I can only wait until this afternoon. You will do well to take me at my word because I don't believe in bluffing. All my past is proof of that.'

To make it all even more impressive, Hitler left Schuschnigg for a few moments and then could be heard shouting for General Keitel (Chief of the German Army High Command), as if he were about to order an invasion of Austria at once! Hitler accompanied all these threats of violence with his demands to Schuschnigg:

> **SOURCE 4.5** What Hitler demanded from Austria (February 1938)
>
> 1 The lifting of the ban on the Austrian Nazi Party
> 2 The appointment of three top Austrian Nazis to lead important ministries in Schuschnigg's government
> 3 Stronger economic and military links between Germany and Austria.

WHAT DO YOU THINK?

1. Make a list *in your own words* of all the sorts of threats that Hitler was making to Schuschnigg.
2. In the circumstances, why do you think Schusschnigg would have had difficulty knowing how to react?

These demands would have effectively meant the end of an independent Austria. Austria would have become a *satellite state* of Germany, and Schuschnigg knew this. However, he had little choice, he had been bullied into submission. He went back to Austria and started obeying Hitler's demands.

On 9th March Schuschnigg changed his mind. He decided to ask the Austrian people themselves if they wanted to remain independent or support a union with Germany. On 9th March he therefore ordered a *plebiscite* to be held on 12th March. This was open defiance of Hitler and he was outraged.

The historian A.J.P. Taylor noted that

> **SOURCE 4.6**
>
> 'Hitler responded as though someone had trodden on a painful corn. He had received no warning and made no preparation . . . He must either act or be humiliated.'

He threatened to take military action (and German troop movements around border areas with Austria made this seem more than a bluff) and he made more demands:

> **SOURCE 4.7** What Hitler demanded from Austria (March 1938)
>
> 1 The cancellation of the plebiscite
> 2 The resignation of Schuschnigg
> 3 The appointment of Seyss-Inquart as Chancellor of Austria

The Austrian government realised there was no one to turn to and gave way to these demands. The Austrian Nazi leader, Seyss-Inquart was appointed as Chancellor and his first act was to send a telegram to Berlin asking for German help *'to restore law and order'*. This meant that when the German tanks and military columns rolled over the Alpine passes into Austria on 12th March, they were not technically invading since they had been invited. It was probably a good job that they did not have to fight their way in since the whole thing was a shambles. 70% of the German vehicles broke down on the road to Vienna. They had so little fuel they were filling up at petrol stations on the main roads, and the tank commander was using a Baedecker tourist guide to plan his route!

Hitler visited Austria on 12th March and was so pleased with his welcome that he decided to go for a full *Anschluss* (rather than just controlling Austria through a 'tame' Nazi government). Therefore, on 13th March the new Austrian government passed a law stating that Austria was now part of the German Reich. On 10th April, the Austrian people were asked to vote on this new arrangement and 99% of the population voted in favour of it, probably a genuine reflection of German feeling.

It is difficult to disagree with the historian Seaman's view that:

SOURCE 4.8

'Hitler had acted impulsively and in a bad temper but he had won a major victory and won it on the cheap.'

WHAT DO YOU THINK?

1. A historian wrote that the *Anschluss* *'Was a striking example of Hitler's ability to combine patient preparation with opportunism and improvisation in execution.'* Can you find evidence of Hitler's patience, his preparation, his 'taking his chance' and 'thinking fast on his feet' when you consider Hitler's conduct during the Anschluss?

2. Do you agree with Seaman's view in Source 4.8 that Hitler had *'won it on the cheap'*?

SOURCE 4.9 *Photograph of German troops in Vienna 1938*

THE BRITISH REACTION: FAVOURABLE

Neville Chamberlain had become Prime Minister in May 1937. He wanted to improve relations with Germany and in November 1937, had sent Lord Halifax to Germany to attend meetings with German leaders. At these discussions, Halifax laid out Britain's position – she would do nothing to interfere with any German plans in Central Europe.

This is well summed up by Chamberlain himself in one of his letters to his sister.

SOURCE 4.10

'I don't see why we shouldn't say to Germany, give us satisfactory promises that you won't use force to deal with the Austrians and Czechoslovakians and we will give you similar promises that we won't use force to prevent the changes you want, if you can get them by peaceful means.'

It is difficult to imagine a clearer signal to Hitler that he was being given a free hand over Austria, and this lack of interest shown by Chamberlain summed up the attitude of the British government towards the *Anschluss*. Britain considered that the problem of Austria fell within Germany's sphere of interest and that there was no reason for Britain to intervene. The general feeling in Britain was that Schuschnigg had brought the crisis upon himself (by his stupidity in ordering the plebiscite), that Austrians were really Germans so the British government should not stand in their way, and lastly, that it was not Britain's business anyway. *The Daily Mail* on 12th March wrote:

SOURCE 4.11

'Not one British soldier, not one penny of British money, must be involved in a quarrel which is no concern of ours.'

Some were even able to look on the bright side and see the advantages of what had happened. In a letter to *The Times*, a Conservative MP wrote:

SOURCE 4.12

'If the Austrian people had not welcomed this union, they would have fought Germany over it. The fact that there has not been any resistance proves the desire of the two nations to obtain the Anschluss. Austria has free markets for her raw materials and manufactured goods … and more importantly, she is no longer a source of friction in international relations …'

However, most people could see the nonsense of Hitler's claim that Germany had joined with Austria by *'peaceful evolution'*. It was widely recognised that Austria had basically been brutally told 'join or else!'

So, where there was any general complaint, it was usually about

SOURCE 4.13

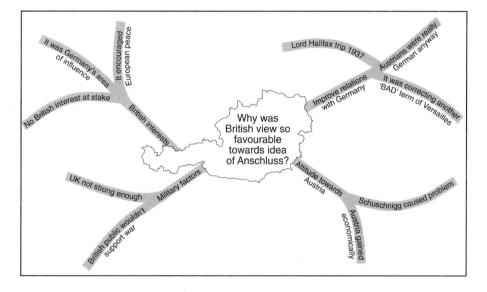

It was Germany's area of influence

It encouraged European peace

No British interest at stake

British interests

Lord Halifax trip 1937

Austrians were really German anyway

Improve relations with Germany

It was correcting another 'BAD' term of Versailles

Why was British view so favourable towards idea of Anschluss?

Attitude towards Austria

UK not strong enough

Military factors

British public wouldn't support war

Schuschnigg caused problem

Austria gained economically

the *methods* that Germany had used to achieve *Anschluss* with Austria.

The Times on 15th March wrote:

SOURCE 4.14

'The use of violent means, under any conditions, to obtain even a legitimate end, is bound to make the British Government and people have natural feelings of resentment.'

On 11 April, *The Times* added:

SOURCE 4.15

'Apart from the methods by which it was achieved, there has never been any public opposition in England to this union of Austria and Germany.'

QUESTION PRACTICE

(See pages 93–99 for advice on different types of questions)

SOURCE 4.16 Cabinet minutes, reporting what Neville Chamberlain said, 12th March 1938.

The manner in which the German action in Austria has been brought about was most distressing and shocking to the world and was a typical example of power politics. This made

international appeasement more difficult … In spite of all however, he felt this thing had to come. Nothing short of an overwhelming display of force could have stopped it. At any rate, the question was now out of the way.

1 Why did Chamberlain refuse to take action over the Anschluss?   *(Outcome 2 – 4 marks)*

          (Use the source and recall)

QUESTION PRACTICE

2 How far do Chamberlain's views agree with those of *The Times*?   *(Outcome 3 – 3 marks)*

          (Use Sources 4.14, 4.15, 4.16)

3 Describe the events which led to Germany's annexation of Austria in 1938.

          (Outcome 2 – 4 marks)

THE BRITISH REACTION: UNFAVOURABLE

There were only a few in Britain who stood out against the *Anschluss*. The most outstanding and perceptive critic of Government policy was Winston Churchill.

He had a very pessimistic view of things and his speech in the House of Commons showed this . . .

SOURCE 4.17

'The seriousness of the events of the German annexation of Austria cannot be exaggerated. Europe is faced with a programme of aggression and there is only one choice open; either to submit like Austria or else to take effective measures while time remains, to defend ourselves from danger . . .

If we do not do this, where will we be two years from now, when the German army will certainly be much larger than the French army, and when all the small nations will have left the League of Nations to join the ever growing power of the Nazi system, and to make the best deal that they can?'

Churchill had no time for the widely held view that it was a long way away and none of Britain's business.

Churchill's view was echoed by the Shepard cartoon, Source 4.18, which shows the smaller states sitting in a row looking nervous. Austria has already gone, Czechoslovakia is next. There doesn't seem much they can do to resist what will happen to them.

SOURCE 4.18 *Cartoon by Shepard from* Punch

Churchill also pointed out some other disadvantages that were caused by Germany annexing Austria and making it a part of the German Reich. His speech continued:

SOURCE 4.19

'... *There are some things I have not seen brought out in the press. Vienna is the centre of communications of the old Austro-Hungarian Empire and all the countries in the south east of Europe. A long stretch of the River Danube is now in German hands. Nazi Germany now has military and economic control of all the routes into Southeastern Europe, by road, by river, by rail ...*'

WHAT DO YOU THINK?

Why was Churchill so worried about the *Anschluss*?

Most of the British press didn't really oppose the *Anschluss*, but there were some newspapers which were prepared to consider what lessons could be learnt from it. Most took on board the message that Britain should do something to improve its own military strength. *The Observer's* view was that:

SOURCE 4.20

'*The lesson is that the British people, while absolutely refusing to be involved in Eastern Europe this time, should extend their rearmament without delay ...*'

This opinion was echoed by *The Times* which wrote:

SOURCE 4.21

'*The British government will see first and foremost to its own armaments – that is clearly what matters most.*'

THE INTERNATIONAL REACTION TO THE ANSCHLUSS

ITALY

It might have been thought that Italy would be most upset by Germany's annexation of Austria. After all, only four years earlier, Mussolini had been in a strong enough position to fight to put Hitler off any idea of a take-over at the time of Dollfuss' assassination. Now, however, there was little Mussolini could do; Germany was far too strong and had widespread support inside Austria for its actions.

The Italian foreign minister, Ciano, showed a fine sense of realism on this point when he wrote:

SOURCE 4.22

'*What in fact could we do? Start a war with Germany? At the first shot we fired, every Austrian, without exception, would fall in behind the Germans against us.*'

Curiously, Hitler himself *was* worried about Italy's position. He may have had anxieties that he had over-stepped himself by pushing ahead with the 'invasion' plan without clearing it with Mussolini. When Mussolini sent Hitler a message saying that *'Austria did not interest him at all'*, Hitler was full of gratitude (and emotional relief), saying:

SOURCE 4.23

'Tell Mussolini I will never forget this ... never, never, never ... whatever may happen. If he should ever need help or be in danger, he can be convinced I shall stick to him ...'

CZECHOSLOVAKIA

Germany feared Czech intervention till the last moment and went to some lengths to calm them. Goering told the Czech minister: *'I give you my word of honour that Czechoslovakia has not the least reason to feel any anxiety'*. They didn't believe him since one look at the new map showed that Czechoslovakia now stood out like a sore thumb sticking into Germany, surrounded on three sides and their northern frontier defences now useless. They were in a perilous strategic position, but what could they do?

FRANCE

As usual it seemed, France was in the middle of changing governments; the last government had fallen three days before and therefore no one was in a position to take responsibility for any action over the *Anschluss*. However, a German diplomat, Franz von Papen had already noted that French ministers:

SOURCE 4.24

'... considered a change in the direction of French policy in Central Europe as entirely open to discussion ... and they had no objection to a marked extension of German influence in Austria, obtained through evolutionary means.'

In other words, France's view on matters in Austria was no different from that of Britain. The international community was therefore broadly in agreement, that nothing either should or could be done, in response to Germany taking over Austria. It does seem curious that, as the breaches of the Versailles terms got bigger and the stakes got higher, it in fact seemed easier for Hitler to get away with them!

WHAT DO YOU THINK?

Why did Hitler worry about Italy and Czechoslovakia and not about France?

THE EFFECTS OF GERMANY'S ACTION IN ANNEXING AUSTRIA

There were many different areas where Germany gained because of the Anschluss with Austria.

ECONOMIC

As W. Carr noted:

SOURCE 4.25

'The economic advantages of Anschluss were far from negligible. Some additional steel capacity and ore mines... fell into German hands, also Austria's foreign exchange reserves (440 million Reichmarks)'

PERSONAL

It confirmed in Hitler's mind the idea that his policies were a fulfilment of destiny. In his speech on 9th April 1938, he said:

SOURCE 4.26

'I believe it is God's will to send a youth from here to the Reich, to let him grow up, to raise him to be a leader of the nation so as to enable him to lead back his homeland into the Reich.'

MILITARY

Germany's population increased with the addition of seven million Austrians, which included their army of 100 000 men. Germany was now in control of Vienna and this gave it a much stronger position in the Balkans.

ON THE INTERNATIONAL COMMUNITY

European statesmen began to doubt if Hitler could ever be trusted; some wondered if the policy of appeasement really was the best idea. Although Chamberlain himself didn't budge from his feeling that his policy of appeasement was right, even he was forced to admit in his speech to Parliament, that his hopes had suffered a severe jolt by Hitler's actions over Austria. He said ...

SOURCE 4.27

'It is quite untrue that we have ever given Germany our encouragement to absorb Austria into the German Reich.... It has always been made plain that we would strongly disapprove of solving these problems by violent means. The hard fact is that nothing could have stopped Germany unless we had been prepared to use force to prevent it.

We strongly condemn the methods Germany has used, and admit that we, and all those interested in preserving European peace, have been profoundly shocked.'

Some newspapers expressed the same doubts about continuing to deal with Hitler. *The Glasgow Herald* held the view that:

SOURCE 4.28

'In this matter, the rights and wrongs of the Anschluss itself are beside the point. What alone matters is the attitude of Nazi Germany towards the promises its *leader makes and their lack of sincerity in dealing with friendly governments like our own. Should we not lay down a limit beyond which we shall not be prepared to allow the forcible remaking of Europe to proceed?'*

So, as the historian William Rock put it:

SOURCE 4.29

'*Chamberlain accepted that conversations with Hitler must be set aside for some time, but he was hopeful that, if another violent coup in Czechoslovakia could be avoided, which he thought possible, Europe might settle down again and peace talks be resumed with the Germans. So, the independence and integrity of Austria, officially upheld in former years as a vital element of European peace, was given away in the name of appeasement.*'

The question now was, if Czechoslovakia did become the next item of Hitler's shopping list, would that be given away in the name of appeasement also?

WHAT DO YOU THINK?

1 Why was the *Anschluss* such a bonus for Germany?
2 How fully does Source 4.31 explain the main effects of the *Anschluss* on the international community?
3 What two points does the Glasgow Herald make about the future peace of Europe?

QUESTION PRACTICE

(See pages 93–99 for advice on different types of questions)

SOURCE 4.30 Neville Chamberlain speaking in the House of Commons on 8th April 1938. Parliament was discussing the German take-over of Austria.

Our policy is not to divide Europe into opposing blocks of countries, arming against each other and heading for war. That seems to us a policy which is dangerous and stupid. You may say we do not approve of dictators. We cannot remove them. We have to live with them. We should take any and every opportunity to try to remove any genuine grievances that may exist.

1 Why did Chamberlain appease Germany over Austria in 1938?

(Outcome 2 – 4 marks)

(Use the above source and recall)

SOURCE 4.31 Lord Tweedsmuir on 15th March 1938

'*I don't see what the problem is. Austria will be much happier as a part of Germany. The Treaty of Versailles said that Germany and Austria must never unite but that treaty was foolish. Some people will say that if Germany gets Austria then Czechoslovakia will be Hitler's next target, but that's not our problem.*

2 How fully does this source explain the British reaction to the German annexation of Austria?

(Outcome 2 – 4 marks)

(Use the source and recall)

5

THE ROAD TO MUNICH: THE CZECHOSLOVAKIAN CRISIS 1938

This chapter will do four main things:
◆ explain the background to Hitler's policy towards Czechoslovakia
◆ describe the events of 1938 in Czechoslovakia, leading to the Munich Agreement
◆ discuss the British and international reaction to the Munich Agreement
◆ weigh up the effects of Germany's action in occupying the Sudetenland

INTRODUCTION

Czechoslovakia was one of the new states created by the peace treaties of 1919, out of the wreckage of the old Austro-Hungarian Empire. The new state had a population of 14 million. Half of these were Czechs, then there were two million Slovaks, three million Sudeten Germans and smaller groups of Magyars, Rumanians and Poles. Its founding president was Thomas Masaryk, and he had established a parliamentary republic with wide democratic rights. It had a surprisingly strong industrial sector for such a small country (world's sixth largest industrial employer and seventh largest arms manufacturer) and this helped support an effective army of 34 divisions. It was generally accepted that Czechoslovakia was one of the success stories of the 1919 peace settlement. It had become a strong, proud and free state in the middle of Europe and had been given some security by a system of military alliances with France and Russia. Since 1935 its leader was President Edward Benes.

SOURCE 5.1 *Map of Czechoslovakia*

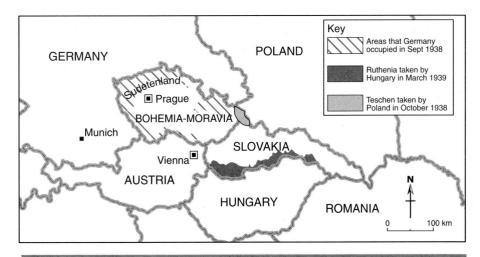

THE BACKGROUND TO HITLER'S POLICY TOWARDS CZECHOSLOVAKIA

Hitler's attitude towards Czechoslovakia was shaped by many different factors.
◆ *Versailles.* Czechoslovakia had been created by the Treaty of St

Germain (which dealt with the Austrian Empire), but Hitler lumped it in with the hated Treaty of Versailles (which dealt only with Germany). Hitler is claimed to have called Czechoslovakia *'That bastard child of Versailles'*. It was a constant reminder to the German government and people of the humiliation of their punishment at Versailles. It was one of the biggest creations of Versailles in the European area that had an impact on Germany (Poland of course was the other).

♦ *Sudetenland*. The old Austrian empire contained many different nationalities, including over three million German-speaking Sudetenlanders. They had *never* belonged to Germany and it was not as if they had been conquered in some previous age by the Austrian Empire (although Chamberlain talked of them, as if he were somehow 'returning' them to their homeland). As the peacemakers of 1919 dealt with the disintegrated Austrian Empire, the problem had arisen as to what to do with the Sudetenlanders. They were German speaking, and to some extent considered themselves as German, but it was decided that they could not be placed within Germany's borders, simply because that would have been rewarding Germany for losing the war by making her bigger! They were therefore placed within the boundaries of the new state of Czechoslovakia. Hitler referred to all German speakers outside Germany's borders as the *Auslandsdeutsch*, and wanted them brought back within the borders of the German homeland, into what was called the *Volksgemeinschaft* (people's community).

♦ *Lebensraum*. We have already mentioned Hitler's policy of looking for extra living space for the German population. This was to come from the open lands in the east of Europe. One problem of Hitler's *Drang Nach Osten* policy (the Drive to the East) was that Czechoslovakia stood in the way. If Germany could control Czechoslovakia, then implementing the *Lebensraum* policy would become much easier.

♦ *Austria*. It is unlikely that Hitler had any immediate plans in 1938 to make a 'bid' for Czechoslovakia. After all, the timetable of the Hossbach Memorandum had indicated 1944 for Czechoslovakia, and anyway, in early 1938 Hitler was pre-occupied with Austria. However, his success in Austria possibly led to him conclude that the same could be achieved with Sudetenland, at an earlier date than 1944. Also, the Austrian success had stirred up the Sudetenlanders into thinking that it would be their turn next to be welcomed into the Greater German Reich. It cost Hitler little to encourage a little bit of de-stabilisation of Czechoslovakia, to see what would come out of it. . . .

WHAT DO YOU THINK?

❶ What was there about Czechoslovakia that made it like Western European states?

❷ What factors had an influence on the way Hitler thought about Czechoslovakia?

THE EVENTS OF 1938 IN CZECHOSLOVAKIA, LEADING TO THE MUNICH AGREEMENT

The success in Austria had been partly brought about by Hitler's 'agents working within', the de-stabilising work of the Austrian Nazi Party. Hitler had a similar advantage inside Czechoslovakia. Since the early 1930s there had been in Sudetenland a strong and active Czech Nazi party called the Sudeten German Party (SDP). Its leader was Konrad Henlein. They were financed and controlled by the German Nazi Party. Simply speaking, their orders were to keep complaining that the Sudeten Germans were being persecuted, and make demands that could not be satisfied by the Czechoslovakian government. That would make the Sudeten Germans look like the victims, and therefore anything that Germany did by way of later intervention would look like they were rescuing a persecuted minority.

In April 1938 Henlein issued the 8-point Karlsbad Programme. This was a set of demands for virtual *autonomy* of Sudetenland from the Czechoslovakian state.

WHAT DO YOU THINK?

1. What was the policy that Henlein's Sudeten German Party were going to follow over the Sudetenland?
2. Why did this policy suit Germany?

The way Britain and France saw the problem of Czechoslovakia was like this: What would happen if the Czechoslovakian government *refused* to give way to Sudeten demands and, for instance, imposed military law on the Sudetenland to keep them in order? Wouldn't that be just about asking Germany to send troops in to protect their fellow Sudeten Germans? That would surely then commit Britain and France to going to war to defend Czechoslovakia? It was a terrible situation to be in. Chamberlain was horrified at the awful prospect of being dragged into a war that was not of Britain's making.

It was Chamberlain's determination not to be dragged into an unnecessary war that influenced his policy for the next six months. It also led to what he thought was a clever policy. He believed *the Czechs were the problem*, so they had to be made to give way. But the issue was a German problem also. If the Czechs gave way too easily, the Germans might start asking for even more. *Both* sides would have to be made to compromise. Chamberlain's solution was to follow a policy whereby he would convince the Czechs that Britain would not intervene, whilst at the same time convince the Germans that Britain would. This would drive them both to the negotiating table and the matter could be settled. In fact, this policy was so unclear, it merely meant that neither the Czechs nor the Germans really knew where Britain stood and therefore did *not* help prevent the crisis.

WHAT DO YOU THINK?

1. Why were events in the Sudetenland of such concern to Britain and France?
2. What was Chamberlain's policy to settle the problems over the Sudetenland?

THE MAY CRISIS 1938

On the weekend of 20–21 May, the Czech army partially _mobilised_ . German troops movements had been reported in frontier areas and in a highly militarised country like Germany, it was impossible to move troops around without giving someone the impression that an attack was likely somewhere. The Czechoslovakian government assumed an attack was aimed at them and went to a state of alert. Britain and France in their turn, warned Germany against the aggression and the crisis died down.

Two effects of this crisis are worth mentioning:

1 The whole crisis had probably been created by the Czechs over-reacting, since the Germans never really had planned troop movements as a rehearsal for Case Green (the operational invasion of Czechoslovakia as proposed in the Hossbach Memorandum of 1937). The effect of the crisis though, was that Hitler was enraged by his apparent humiliation; it looked like he had been made to back down. This caused him to change his plan so that Czechoslovakia now did become his next target for conquest, _as soon as possible._ On 28th May he told his senior generals that it was his unshakeable will that Czechoslovakia should be wiped off the map. He also gave them a deadline date of 1st October 1938.

2 Britain and France drew two conclusions from the episode. Firstly that their firmness had 'saved the day' and that if they stayed firm with Hitler, then he could be made to come to an agreement over Czechoslovakia. The second conclusion was that it confirmed in the mind of the British government that the Czechs were to blame and that Czechoslovakia must be forced to make major concessions, which would be enough to deter Hitler from going to war at some time in the future.

SOURCE 5.2 _Cartoon by Low_

WHAT'S CZECHOSLOVAKIA TO ME, ANYWAY ?

These two points are the key features which help explain the events that occurred over the rest of the summer of 1938. On the one hand Hitler continued to 'crank up' tension to make Czechoslovakia more vulnerable. On the other hand, Britain pursued a policy that had the effect of undermining and weakening Czechoslovakia. Germany was looking for reasons to attack Czechoslovakia, while Britain was looking for reasons not to defend it. It rather came to the same thing in the end.

WHAT DO YOU THINK?

1. Explain the view of Low's cartoon, Source 5.2, on Britain's attitude towards the developing Czechoslovakian crisis during the summer of 1938.

THE BEHAVIOUR OF BRITAIN, GERMANY AND CZECHOSLOVAKIA OVER THE SUMMER OF 1938

BRITAIN

In July, Chamberlain sent Lord Runciman to Czechoslovakia as a *mediator* to look at the Sudeten problem. If he could delay things a bit, that would probably be useful, but his real job was to come up with a list of concessions that he could persuade the Czech President Benes to agree to. He therefore tended to sympathise with the grievances of the Sudeten Germans.

GERMANY

Hitler continued to encourage the Sudeten Germans to keep agitating in order to keep the situation there unstable. The German army organised large-scale military exercises in Germany in July and partial mobilisation of its armed forces by August. Hitler made vague diplomatic statements, aimed at Hungary and Poland, to encourage them to think that they could get bits of territory from Czechoslovakia also, if things went favourably for them (Poland wanted the area of Teschen, while Hungary desired Eastern Ruthenia).

CZECHOSLOVAKIA

How was Czechoslovakia going to react to all this going on around them? On 4th September Benes made proposals that threatened to defuse the whole situation. He called a meeting with Henlein and the Sudeten German party and promised them everything they had demanded in the Karlsbad Programme. This, of course, was precisely *not* what they had wanted. The freeing of the Sudetenland was not what they had really been after, that was merely the issue to be exploited by Germany in order to go to war with Czechoslovakia. President Benes' offer had removed that whole excuse. The Sudeten Germans promptly broke off negotiations.

On 12th September, Hitler gave a violent address at a Nuremberg rally and made alarming threats of intervention in Czechoslovakia. Hitler ranted and raved about the oppressed Sudeten Germans and demanded justice for them. He called them *'those poor tortured creatures'* and personally insulted President Benes. Hitler was deliberately stirring things up, to see what would come of it.

Riots in the Sudetenland, touched off by Hitler's speech, led to the imposition of *martial law* by the Czech authorities. War looked imminent and the French, who would be the first to be dragged in, panicked. Their Prime Minister Daladier and Foreign minister Bonnet flew to London, looking for Britain's advice on how to avoid the situation turning into open war. Bonnet believed that the question of peace or war was not even a matter of days, but a matter of minutes!

Chamberlain had already decided, possibly before the end of August, that only his personal intervention could drag Europe back from the brink of war. He said, *'I thought of a plan, so unconventional, it took Halifax's breath away'*. His plan was to fly to Germany to talk to Hitler, and on 13th September he informed Hitler

SOURCE 5.3

'In view of the increasingly critical situation I propose to come over at once to see you with a view of trying to find a peaceful solution.'

WHAT DO YOU THINK?

1. Describe the different attitudes and behaviour of Britain, Germany and Czechoslovakia towards the Sudeten Crisis? Which state do you think most wanted to settle the crisis?

2. What was Chamberlain's personal view of the Sudeten problem by September 1938?

NEVILLE CHAMBERLAIN'S THREE MEETINGS

In the last fortnight of September 1938 there was an incredible flurry of diplomatic activity involving Chamberlain and his peace-making attempts. He attended three meetings with Hitler, which started on three consecutive Thursdays, although some lasted more than that one day and they were in three different places in Germany.

MEETING I BERCHTESGADEN 15TH SEPTEMBER

The first meeting between Hitler and Chamberlain was held at the Berghof in Berchtesgaden (the same venue as the ill-fated meeting between Schuschnigg and Hitler in February 1938!). Chamberlain flew there (the first time this 69 year old statesman had ever flown) and he took two foreign office advisors with him (but didn't have them present during the talks). He took no interpreter although he spoke no German himself, and Hitler spoke no English. Since Chamberlain had already decided what he was going to do anyway, it is possible there was no need for an interpreter. Hitler demanded an instant solution to the Sudetenland problem, and Chamberlain agreed that he was prepared to break up Czechoslovakia and give away the Sudetenland, without actually asking the Czechs. He told Hitler:

SOURCE 5.4

'In principle I have nothing to say against the separation of Sudetenland from the rest of Czechoslovakia, provided that the practical difficulties could be overcome.'

WHAT DO YOU THINK?

① Why do you think it needed some *'intense bullying'* to get the Czechs to accept? (Think of the difference between the Karlsbad Programme and the Berchtesgaden terms).

② Study Source 5.5 What is its view of Chamberlain's diplomatic behaviour? (Remember to consider caption, date and features of the illustration that help you to place it in its historical context.)

SOURCE 5.5 *Cartoon from* Punch

STILL HOPE

He agreed that any Sudeten areas with over 50% German population were to be given to Germany. Hitler agreed to give Chamberlain time to discuss this idea with France who, with Britain, would have to persuade Czechoslovakia to accept it. This was not, of course, really what Hitler wanted since it denied him the chance to destroy Czechoslovakia, but it was an offer too good to turn down. Chamberlain flew back to London and in a week of hard discussion he convinced the French government to support the plan and, with some intense bullying, the Czechoslovakian government were forced to accept the terms.

MEETING 2 GODESBERG 22ND SEPTEMBER

Chamberlain must have been fairly satisfied with the way events were progressing when he flew off to meet Hitler for the second time. The collapse of any Czech opposition to his plans must have given him genuine hope that he stood on the brink of establishing European peace.

He made this point himself, as he said at Heston airport, before setting off:

SOURCE 5.6

'European peace is what I am aiming at, and I hope this journey may open the way to get it.'

He may also have been flattered by Hitler's agreement to meet him at Godesberg, (on the Rhine) which was a far shorter flight. As Hitler had said, he wanted to save the travels of an old man!

At the Godesberg meeting, Chamberlain got a shock; with a brief word of apology, Hitler rejected all Chamberlain's hard won concessions. Hitler told him *'I am sorry but that is not enough.'* He had raised the stakes. He told Chamberlain that Sudeten Germans were being massacred by Czech forces (a lie) and that he must send in the German army to stop that immediately. He wanted to occupy the Sudetenland and it was to be handed over in its present condition with no compensation for lost Czech property or belongings (by 28th September at the latest). Also he was aware that Poland and Hungary wanted to protect the interests of their oppressed minorities inside the Czech border and must be allowed to do so. Hitler ended by saying:

SOURCE 5.7

'The Czech problem is the last territorial demand I have to make in Europe.'

Chamberlain was staggered by these new claims and told Hitler the lengths he personally had gone to preserve European peace. *The Times* reported Chamberlain's words:

SOURCE 5.8

'He had persuaded his colleagues, the French and the Czechs, to agree in principle to self-determination, in fact he had got exactly what the Fuhrer wanted

without the expenditure of a drop of German blood. In doing so, he had been obliged to put his political reputation on the line. He was accused of selling the Czechs, yielding to dictators, surrendering and so on. He had actually been booed on his departure today.'

Chamberlain telephoned Halifax (his foreign secretary) and told him *'his interview with Hitler had been most unsatisfactory'*. Halifax's reply was possibly designed to put a bit of backbone into Chamberlain. Halifax told him:

SOURCE 5.9

'... it seems of vital importance that you should not leave without making it plain to the Chancellor, if possible by special interview, that after the great concessions made by the Czech government, for him to reject the opportunity of peaceful solution in favour of one which must involve war, would be an unforgivable crime against humanity.'

These were strong words from Halifax who normally gave Chamberlain his total support, but who was now maybe beginning to see *'the folly of endless, unqualified appeasement.'*

Chamberlain was very discouraged. He could see that Hitler was a man who was looking for a fight over Czechoslovakia; that the point of these excessive demands was precisely so that they had to be turned down, so that Hitler could then declare war.

SOURCE 5.10 *Cartoon by Low*

"MEIN KAMPF"

The point was made in the last chapter (and the Low cartoon) about the difficulty that conventional diplomats and statesmen had in dealing with Hitler. They couldn't see how he could behave the way he did because they couldn't understand his attitude to war. As W. Carr put it:

WHAT DO YOU THINK?

As we have seen, Cartoons are often very clever ways of summing up a situation. The following cartoon by Low was published **just after** Chamberlain returned from Godesberg. It is critical of Chamberlain, but also in some ways sympathises with him.

Can you make a comment on:
a the meaning/significance of the caption?
b the condition of and the writing on the two angels at the front?
c Chamberlain's appearance, position and the folder under his arm?

If you can comment on these three aspects, you will have covered the main points that Low was trying to make. You would also be able to answer an Examination question like: How well does this source sum up Chamberlain's problems in bringing peace to Europe?

'War was not a sign of bankrupt statesmanship to the Fuhrer or a hopeless plunge into the irrational but, on the contrary, a sign of national strength and a natural part of the struggle for existence ... That instinctive hatred of war which was widespread in the western democracies and their leaders was totally lacking in Hitler.'

One can't help thinking that if Chamberlain had been able to grasp an understanding of this idea in his opponent, he may have behaved differently.

Chamberlain returned to London on Saturday 24th September, and he told the Cabinet the following day that Hitler's Godesberg proposals should be accepted. The Cabinet gave Chamberlain a shock when it collectively over-rode him and refused to agree. They had decided enough was enough and they would rather risk war than put pressure on Czechoslovakia to accept the Godesberg terms.

At 5pm on Sunday the Czechs delivered their own reply to the British government concerning the Godesberg proposals. It was delivered by Jan Masaryk, the Czech minister in London and son of the founding President.

SOURCE 5.12

'The British and French governments are well aware that we agreed under the most severe pressure to the Anglo-French plan for giving up parts of Czechoslovakia ... we accepted because we understood that it was the end of the demands to be made upon us. Yesterday, after the return of Mr Chamberlain from Godesberg, a new offer was handed to my government ... it is an ultimatum of the sort usually presented to a defeated nation and not an offer to a sovereign state that has shown the greatest possible readiness to make sacrifices for the appeasement of Europe. My government is amazed at the contents of the memorandum ... they take away from us every safeguard for our national existence.

My government declares that Herr Hitler's demands in their present form are totally unacceptable to my government. Against these new and cruel demands my government feel bound to make their utmost resistance and with God's help, we shall do so.'

It is worth putting this document in at some length. It contains moving language, combined with a sense of honour, integrity and resolve. In a dignified way, the Czechs were now telling the British government, 'We have had enough, we are going to make a fight of it even if you keep letting us down'

The possibility of war was looming again and the last days of September were nervous ones. The Czechs had mobilised their army, the French government had called up military reservists and the British had mobilised their fleet and warned anti-aircraft batteries to be in a state of readiness.

On 27th September Chamberlain made a famous wireless speech to the British public, saying:

SOURCE 5.14 Daily Mirror *newspaper front page*

SOURCE 5.15

WHAT DO YOU THINK?

1. Why do you think Chamberlain was always at a disadvantage when dealing with Hitler?

2. Study Jan Masaryk's letter and explain what the Czechs were talking about after they had heard the Godesberg proposals?

3. Look at Source 5.15. What view does it hold about Britain's attitude towards the Czechoslovakian problem. [Remember the drill to break the cartoon down into different bits you can explain].

SOURCE 5.13

'How horrible, fantastic, incredible it is that we should be digging trenches and trying on gas masks here because of a quarrel in a far away country between people of whom we know nothing.'

Historians now tend to see these as ill-judged and *scaremongering* words by Chamberlain (after all, Germany had no bombers capable of flying from Germany to Britain and back to drop these bombs). But on the morning of 28th September the inhabitants of British towns expected to endure German bombing within days or even hours.

The fact was, however, that the German bombing of Britain was *not* going to happen in 1938, because Hitler had already changed his mind about what he was going to do. It was Hitler who edged away from the precipice. What made him change his mind?

- He had not received the expected enthusiastic welcome from the German population for his plans to occupy Czechoslovakia. He had been angered by the sparse and silent crowds watching troop movements in Berlin. They had liked getting Austria for nothing but this time it looked like a war.

- The British and French seemed to be backing up the Czechs. The French had started a very efficient mobilisation. Hitler's intuition told him that they would, in the end, back down, but just maybe they wouldn't. Perhaps it would be better to ease off and not 'push' so strongly.

- By mid-day of 28th September, Hitler was filled with growing doubts about the advisability of turning the Czech crisis into a full-scale war. At that moment a message arrived from the Italian leader Mussolini urging the same caution. Mussolini suggested that he would chair a four-power conference to see if an agreement over Czechoslovakia could be reached. When the offer of a conference was made, Hitler therefore agreed to go. The conference would be held the next day in Munich.

WHAT DO YOU THINK?

What factors influenced Hitler to move away from starting a war over Czechoslovakia in September 1938?

SOURCE 5.16 *The Munich conference*

MEETING 3 MUNICH 29TH SEPTEMBER

The Munich Conference was attended by Chamberlain (Britain), Daladier (France) and Hitler (Germany), and chaired by Mussolini (Italy). There was no invitation to Czechoslovakia, their spokesmen sat outside on the steps. Nor was Russia invited. There were nine hours of negotiations in which Mussolini presented the Godesberg terms for discussion (as if they were a new set of proposals) and everyone then agreed to them. The only difference was that Czechoslovakia was given 12 hours to accept them and ten days to implement them (this was considered an improvement on the word *'immediately'* which had been in the original Godesberg terms!)

The Czech delegates, sitting patiently outside, were shown the terms and told by Daladier *'that this was a sentence without right of appeal and without possibility of modification.'*

Chamberlain may have got part of what he had come to Munich for. After all, this agreement meant there would not be a war over Czechoslovakia. But he knew that when he took the agreement back to Britain, it would be regarded as a betrayal. He needed something else go back with. He still firmly believed that the style of policy he was following, where statesmen discussed things face to face and kept their word so that they knew where they stood, was the right one. If only he could get Hitler to agree in writing that this was the best policy, surely that would be seen as almost a guarantee of future peace. Now that would indeed be a prize worth taking back to tell the British public. Accordingly, Chamberlain had a further meeting with Hitler, in which Chamberlain produced two copies of a pre-prepared statement, which said:

SOURCE 5.17

'We regard the agreement signed last night and the Anglo-German naval agreement as symbolic of the desire of our two peoples never to go to war again. We are resolved that the method of consultation shall be the method adopted to

deal with any other questions that may concern our two countries, and we are determined to continue our efforts to remove possible sources of difference and thus to contribute to assure the peace of Europe.'

Hitler was prepared to sign it. This is what Chamberlain regarded as his *real* achievement when he returned home from Munich. When he got out of the plane, in front of the cheering crowds, he said:

SOURCE 5.18

'The settlement of the Czech problem which has now been achieved is, in my view, only the prelude to a larger settlement in which all Europe may find peace'.

He then waved *'The paper which bears Hitler's name upon it, as well as mine'* and read out its contents. This famously became known as the 'Piece of paper'.

Shortly after the Munich Agreement had been signed by the four powers, its terms were implemented as agreed, with Czechoslovakia being partially broken up. Germany occupied the Sudetenland in October 1938 in what was to be a first instalment on the rest of Czechoslovakia.

WHAT DO YOU THINK?

What was Chamberlain's achievement at Munich?

SOURCE 5.19   *Hitler entering the Sudetenland*

It is well worth studying the 'Munich Crisis' in depth. It is possibly one of the most significant events in twentieth century British diplomatic history, maybe Britain's moment of greatest shame. Even in September 1988, the press, in their 50th anniversary writings, were full of articles by now aged participants, who mused if they couldn't have done something different and more honourable, now that they look back on it. They now accept there was little dignity or honour in the way Britain behaved . . . it was all *expediency*. One wonders why that behaviour should have been unexpected! After all it could have been predicted by the way Britain had behaved over Abyssinia only three years earlier. The Hoare–Laval Pact in 1935 had been a rather dishonourable attempt to divide up Abyssinia without consulting their government, so that Britain and France

SOURCE 5.20 *Chamberlain at Heston airport with the 'Piece of Paper'*

could avoid going to war with Italy. The Munich Agreement was very much just more of the same.

The historian J. Wheeler-Bennett, in the standard work on Munich, summed up the two ways of looking at Britain's discredited policy over Czechoslovakia.

SOURCE 5.21

'Let us admit about the Munich settlement that it could not be avoided; that faced with a lack of preparedness in Britain's armaments and defences, with the collapse of French morale, and with the uncertainty of Russia to fight, Mr Chamberlain had no alternative to do other than he did. Let us pay tribute to his persistence in carrying out what he honestly believed was right. Let us accept and admire all these things, but let us not forget the shame and the humiliation that were ours, let us not forget that, in order to save our skins – we were forced to sacrifice a small power to slavery.'

THE BRITISH AND INTERNATIONAL REACTION TO THE MUNICH AGREEMENT

It is only in the 1990s that discussion on what the British people thought *at the time* of their government's actions in appeasing Hitler has become a key issue of historical debate. Opinion polls were still new in the 1930s, so, with the inconclusive data and unsophisticated sampling methods, it is understandably difficult for historians to come to firm conclusions on what exactly the British public thought about issues of appeasement at that time. In any case, it would naturally be difficult to see shades of changing opinion (e.g. was late 1937 different from mid 1938?) and it is also difficult to quantify opinion (e.g. exactly what percentage of the adult public supported Chamberlain in late September 1938?). Due to the shortcomings in statistical information, historians tended to repeat the views of 1930s newspapers as if they were the best guide to what the British public thought. This, of course, rather innocently assumed that newspapers *reflect* public opinion whereas it has become much clearer that they also *create* it. Historians nowadays

SOURCE 5.22 *Newspaper headlines*

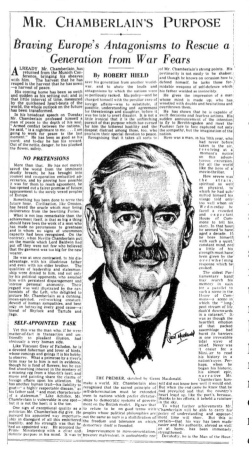

are much more aware of Chamberlain's talents at 'news management', his ability to convince the press (especially *The Times*) to print news in a certain way, to shape it to give a particular impression. Newspapers in the late 1930s (and BBC Radio) therefore tended to give an impression of overwhelming public support for Chamberlain, simply because they never let legitimate opponents of Chamberlain's policies get a say or a look in. When we consider the nature of Britain's reaction to Chamberlain's policies up to and including Munich, historians today don't paint such a rosy picture of joy and triumphant relief as used to be the case.

THE BRITISH REACTION – FAVOURABLE

THE PUBLIC

Even on his route back from the airport, Chamberlain noted that people were shouting themselves hoarse, leaping on the running board of the car, banging on the windows and wanting to shake his hand. On the evening of his return from Munich, Chamberlain addressed cheering crowds outside 10 Downing Street. He told them

SOURCE 5.23

'This is the second time there has come back from Germany to Downing Street, Peace with Honour. I believe it is peace in our time.'

These were the words everyone wanted to hear, and the crowds all sang 'For he's a jolly good fellow.' Extra support for his achievement in averting war came from King George VI, who sent a message saying *'Come straight to Buckingham Palace'*. Within three weeks of Munich he had received more than 20 000 letters and telegrams, some came with gifts. He received scores of fishing rods (people knew his hobby was fly-fishing). There was a widespread sense of public gratitude and relief that his actions had spared Britain another war.

THE PRESS

The press generally fell over itself to praise Chamberlain and play down any doubts or regrets it had about the Munich 'achievement'. The view in *The Times* was that:

SOURCE 5.24

'No conqueror returning from a victory on the battlefield has come home adorned with nobler laurels than Mr Chamberlain from Munich yesterday ... He has found for the nations a new hope for the future ...'

The view that most present historians hold, is that the British press gave a rather deceptive account of the *actual* public response to Chamberlain's deals with Hitler over Czechoslovakia. 'Relief tinged with a large degree of shame' would probably have been more accurate than the widespread picture in the press of enthusiastic gratitude for Chamberlain's statesmanship. As the historians Madge and Harrison commented:

SOURCE 5.25

'During the whole week after Munich, no outsider reading an English newspaper could have guessed that an increasing proportion of the population were feeling once more bewildered, fearful and ashamed.'

BBC

BBC Radio found time to comment on the 5000 supporters of Chamberlain who turned out at Downing Street, but didn't mention the 15 000 counter-demonstrators who turned out in Trafalgar Square. This was only one example of its bias towards supporting Chamberlain, and basically helping to mislead the British population about the true picture of the public response to appeasement. Later, the BBC was to publicly apologise for this aspect of its broadcasting policy in the 1930s.

PARLIAMENT

In the House of Commons there was a four day debate on Munich where much opposition was voiced about the methods and effects of Chamberlain's foreign policy activities. At the end of the debate, Chamberlain received a favourable result of a government majority of 222, but Chamberlain himself realised there were a lot of unhappy MPs who were less convinced of the permanence of his peace deal than he was. Chamberlain himself noted that, *'All the world seems full of my praises except the House of Commons'*.

WHAT DO YOU THINK?

1. What evidence suggests that there was some support for what Chamberlain had achieved at Munich?
2. Why do historians now take great care how they interpret the press evidence about the amount of support for Chamberlain?

THE BRITISH REACTION – UNFAVOURABLE

IN PARLIAMENT

Although Chamberlain had been surprised at the opposition within his cabinet when he returned from Godesberg, only one member of his cabinet resigned in protest over what Chamberlain had done a week later at Munich. Duff Cooper was the First Lord of the Admiralty, and wrote a sad resignation letter that was also highly critical of the ease with which Chamberlain had been duped by Hitler. He wrote:

SOURCE 5.26

'The Prime Minister has confidence in the goodwill and the word of Herr Hitler, although when Herr Hitler broke the Treaty of Versailles, he promised to keep the

Treaty of Locarno, and when he broke the Treaty of Locarno, he undertook not to interfere further, or to have further territorial claims in Europe. When he entered Austria by force, he authorised his henchmen to give an authoritative assurance that he would not interfere with Czechoslovakia. This was less than six months ago. Still the Prime Minister believes that he can rely on the good faith of Hitler. The Prime Minister may be right. I hope and pray that he is right, but I cannot believe what he believes, I wish I could.'

In Parliament itself, during the four day debate, there was time for the opponents of Chamberlain's policy of appeasement to get up and have their say. Most of them were eloquent in their dismissal of any advantages that might have come from the Munich Agreement.

Clement Atlee was leader of the Labour opposition. He said:

SOURCE 5.27

'The events of the last few days are one of the greatest political defeats that this country and France have ever suffered. There can be no doubt that this is a tremendous victory for Herr Hitler. Without firing a shot, just by the threat of military force, he has achieved a dominating position in Europe which Germany failed to win after four years of fighting in the last war. He has destroyed the last home of democracy in Eastern Europe that stood in the way of his ambition. He has opened the way to the food, the oil and the resources that he needs in order to strengthen his military power and he has successfully defeated the forces that might have stood against his rule of violence.'

Archibald Sinclair was the leader of the Liberal Party. He was similarly critical and down-hearted about what Chamberlain had done. He asked:

SOURCE 5.28

'Was it wise of the Prime Minister in his broadcast speech the other night, to talk of quarrels in distant lands between people of whom we know nothing? Shouldn't responsible men try to make people understand the importance to our lives at home, to our standard of living, to the employment of our people and to the protection of our liberties, of distant but important places. We may yet live to regret the day when the government sold the pass of freedom in Central Europe and laid open to German invasion, all the people and resources of Eastern Europe.'

But it was from within his own Conservative Party that the most memorable and elegant condemnation of Chamberlain's policy emerged. When Winston Churchill had a chance to speak, he did not spare Chamberlain. Churchill said:

SOURCE 5.29

'I will begin by saying the most unpopular and unwelcome thing. I will begin by saying what everybody would like to ignore or forget but which nevertheless must be stated, namely that we have suffered a total and unmitigated defeat. The utmost Chamberlain has been able to gain for Czechoslovakia has been that Hitler, instead of snatching the victuals from the table, has been content to have them served to him course by course.

The British people should know that they have passed an awful milestone in our history, when the whole equilibrium of Europe has been deranged and that the terrible words have for the time being been pronounced against the Western democracies, 'Thou art weighed in the balance and found wanting'. And do not suppose that this is the end. This is only the first sip, the first foretaste of a bitter cup that will be proffered to us year by year ... unless we arise and take our stand for freedom.'

SOURCE 5.30 *Cartoon by Low*

OUR NEW DEFENCE

IN THE PRESS

Although the Press itself was generally favourable to Chamberlain, the political cartoonists in the national newspapers surpassed themselves with acute and often damning criticism of what they had seen happening right through the Czechoslovakian crisis. They weren't fooled and they didn't approve of what they saw. Low's cartoon, Source 5.30, printed during the week following Munich, was a cutting criticism of Chamberlain, his methods and all his hopes.

WHAT DO YOU THINK?

1. Think of what Duff Cooper, Atlee, Sinclair, and Churchill said in their speeches. What were all the sorts of objections they expressed to Chamberlain's policy?
2. Analyse the points Low makes in his cartoon and explain why it is so critical of Chamberlain.

THE INTERNATIONAL REACTION

FRANCE

Daladier didn't know what reaction to expect as he flew back to France. When he saw the crowds at the airport, his first thought was that they wanted to lynch him. Then he saw them cheering and realised their relief at avoiding war. He turned to his assistant and said *'the bloody fools'*. However, the French newspaper, *Paris Soir* admired Chamberlain so much that they offered him a *'corner of French soil'* where he might fish.

SOURCE 5.31 *Swiss cartoon on Munich Agreement, 1938*

WIDER EUROPE

Tidens Tegn, a Norwegian newspaper, reckoned the Nobel Prize for Peace should be awarded to Mr Chamberlain. It claimed, '*The whole world agrees that nobody ever did more for peace. The prize was created for men like him*'.

The Dutch obviously agreed with this sentiment and he received 4000 tulips from admirers in Holland.

In Switzerland, their press cartoonists were not so sure that Chamberlain's achievement was so praiseworthy. Source 5.31 quite cleverly shows how they saw, that at Munich, peace [PAX] had been gained by the hidden threat of force.

UNITED STATES

The New York press seemed able to both praise and carefully criticise Chamberlain. The *New York Daily News* went right over the top in their praise, saying:

SOURCE 5.32

'In Chamberlain's actions in the last couple of weeks there is something Christlike ... Chamberlain showed more of the spirit of the founder of Christianity than any English-speaking politician since Abraham Lincoln.'

However, a more thoughtful view was found in the *New York Times*, which realised the cost of Chamberlain's actions (that he had basically sold Czechoslovakia), saying:

SOURCE 5.33

'Let no man say too high a price has been paid for peace in Europe unless he has searched his soul and found himself willing to risk in war the lives of those who are nearest and dearest to him.'

WHAT DO YOU THINK?

One historian wrote that 'The international reaction to Chamberlain's achievement at Munich was mixed.' Does that seem a fair summary?

THE EFFECTS OF GERMANY'S ACTION IN OCCUPYING THE SUDETENLAND

Hitler may have said '*That fellow Chamberlain has ruined my entry into Prague*', but that apart, Germany gained an awful lot at Munich, at almost no cost. In the short run Czechoslovakia lost almost 11 000 square miles (30% of its territory), 30% of its population (including 800,000 Czechs), 50% of its industry including over 90% of its lignite fuel, 55% of its coal and 46% of its electrical energy. Territory went to Poland (Teschen in October 1938) and Hungary (Ruthenia in March 1939).

Czechoslovakia totally lost its strong natural defence line, so the rest of the country became vulnerable to attack.

In the long run, Hitler got his entry to Prague, it was just delayed until March 1939 when the German army marched in and took

Bohemia/Moravia (the western end of the Czech state). The Czechs were in no position to resist and Britain and France did nothing, despite their promise at Munich to protect the rest of Czechoslovakia.

The Czech arms industry then fell into Hitler's hands, including the giant Skoda arms works. Slovakia (the poorer, eastern end of the Czechoslovakian state) was so weak that it just asked Germany if it could become a German protectorate. Hitler had therefore got the whole of Czechoslovakia by March 1939.

Ironically, the fact that Czechoslovakia was given away in 1938–39 meant that Prague was never really in the firing line during the Second World War. Only two bombs fell on it during the war and it was the only European capital to escape almost unscathed from the five years of conflict. If Czechoslovakia had gone to war in 1938 to defend itself, Prague would probably have been flattened.

Another advantage for Germany was that the military balance of power shifted decisively in Germany's favour in Eastern Europe. The German annexation of Austria had made Czechoslovakia weak by making it more open to attack. The taking of Czechoslovakia gave Germany the same advantage over Poland; it could now attack it from different directions. Hitler now commanded the air routes into Poland. His airforce was only 25 minutes flying time from Polish industrial centres.

WHAT DO YOU THINK?

1 What were the economic gains that Germany made from taking over Czechoslovakia?

2 What were the military gains that Germany made from taking over Czechoslovakia?

There was not much comfort that the Western democracies could take from anything they had done over the Czechoslovakian crisis. It could be argued that they had been given another chance to see whether Hitler and the Nazis could keep their word. The evidence now was that they did not keep it. The democracies had finally therefore learned that they could not do business with Hitler and were more determined to stand up to him in the future.

QUESTION PRACTICE

(See pages 93–99 for advice on different types of questions)

SOURCE 5.34 From the diary of Neville Chamberlain on September 19th 1938. He is describing his meeting with Hitler at Berchtesgaden.

For the most part Hitler spoke quietly and in low tones. I did not see any trace of insanity, but occasionally he became very excited and poured out his indignation against the Czechs. I soon saw the situation was more critical than I had thought. I knew that his troops and tanks and planes were ready.

1 How useful is this source in explaining the British government's policies over Czechoslovakia in 1938?

(Outcome 3 – 4 marks)

SOURCE 5.35 The historian Andrew Boxer in his book *Appeasement*:

'Chamberlain believed that Czechoslovakia, because of its mix of nationalities, was an artificial creation that would probably not survive, even without German pressure. It would be futile to go to war to defend it.'

2 Why was Chamberlain not prepared to go to war over Czechoslovakia?

(Outcome 2 – 5 marks)

(Use the source and recall)

SOURCE 5.36 From a letter written by Eleanor Rathbone MP on 30th September 1938

I expect there will be great thanksgiving for peace in the churches tomorrow. On the other hand, there are so many people in whom a sense of relief is quite overcome by an agony of shame over the way the Czechs have been let down.

3 How well does this source sum up the reaction of the British public to the Munich Settlement of September 1938? *(Outcome 3 – 4 marks)*

4 Describe the events of September 1938 which led up to Germany getting the Sudetenland. *(Outcome 2 – 4 marks)*

There is also the possibility of an 8-mark short essay.

Why was the Czechoslovakian Crisis of 1938 so important in international relations?

(Outcomes 1 and 2 – 8 marks)

6

THE FINAL STEPS TO WAR 1938–1939: POLAND

This chapter will do three main things:

◆ explain the background to Hitler's policy over Poland
◆ describe the events between September 1938 and August 1939 leading to the German attack on Poland
◆ discuss the British and French reaction to those events

SOURCE 6.1 *Map of Poland and the surrounding area*

THE BACKGROUND TO HITLER'S POLICY OVER POLAND

Nobody could have believed Hitler when he said that a settlement of the Czechoslovakia problem was his last territorial demand in Europe. It was quite clear that the Treaty of Versailles had created one last outstanding 'problem' that Germany would want to clear up. This was Poland. There were plenty of things about the Polish situation that would have made Hitler want to take action:

1 The terms of Versailles had left the German province of East Prussia split off from Germany by a strip of Polish territory known as the 'Polish Corridor'. Germany wanted to re-unite that province with the main part of Germany.

2 At the end of the 'Corridor' was the city of Danzig, still under League of Nations control but formerly a German town with a German population.

3 Poland had been made economically stronger by including Posen and parts of Silesia. These industrial provinces had been taken from Germany at the Treaty of Versailles, and added to Poland.

4 Hitler regarded it almost as a personal insult that the *Auslandsdeutsch* (a population of about 1.5 million Germans now living in Polish territory) should have been taken away from

Germany and placed under the government of a Slav race that he regarded as so inferior.

5 The vast open areas of Poland were exactly where Hitler had in mind for the operation of his *Lebensraum* policy. To Hitler's way of thinking, the large Jewish population of Poland would be exterminated and the indigenous (Slav) population was only fit to be the servant race to the German settlers who would move in and colonise this area.

Hitler's speech of September 1939 summed up all these grievances:

SOURCE 6.2

'For months we have been suffering under the torture of a problem which the Versailles Diktat created – a problem which has become so bad it is intolerable for us. Danzig was and is a German city. The Corridor was and is German. Both these territories owe their cultural development exclusively to the German people. Danzig was separated from us, the corridor was taken by Poland. As in other German territories of the east, all German minorities living there have been ill-treated in the most distressing manner. More than 1 000 000 people of German blood had in the years 1919–1920 to leave their homeland …'

SOURCE 6.3

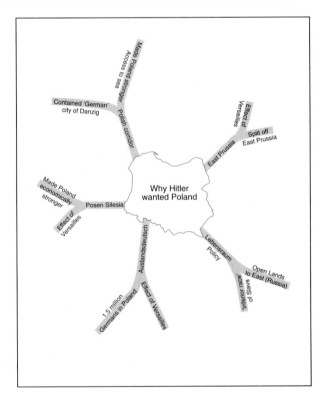

So there are plenty of factors that explain why Hitler had Poland next on his 'shopping list' after Czechoslovakia. He had ordered Case White (the operational military planning to invade Poland) to be prepared in April 1939, and in May he warned his officers:

SOURCE 6.4

'… There is no question of sparing Poland and we are left with the decision to attack Poland at the first opportunity. We cannot expect a repeat of the Czech affair. There will be war this time. Our task is to isolate Poland.'

Hitler would have been right to predict war, because Poland was determined to stick up for itself. Joseph Beck, the Polish Foreign Minister summed it up in a memorandum in March 1939:

SOURCE 6.5

'Hitler might recover a bit of sense once he meets determined opposition, which, up until now he has not met with. The mighty have been humble to him, and the weak have surrendered in advance, even at the cost of their honour. The Germans are marching across Europe with nine divisions; with such strength, Poland will not be overcome ...'

WHAT DO YOU THINK?

1. What did Hitler mean by 'We cannot expect a repeat of the Czech affair'?
2. Explain why you know Beck is referring to the Munich Crisis in the first part of his memo.

THE EVENTS BETWEEN SEPTEMBER 1938– AUGUST 1939 LEADING TO THE GERMAN ATTACK ON POLAND

In mid 1938, Hitler had been worried about the reactions of Britain and France to his plans to take Czechoslovakia. In 1939 he was more worried about Russia in his plans to take Poland. Hitler knew that Germany was strong enough to take on and beat Poland, but was it strong enough to also take on anybody who sided with her? As the year progressed, Hitler could see where Britain and France stood in relation to Poland, but didn't believe they would actually act. (He also couldn't see that they could do anything that would actually make a difference since they were so far away!) It was a bigger worry to Hitler what Russia might do; she might feel very threatened by a German attack on Poland. Russia also had a mutual assistance pact with France (1936) which might bring France into a war to help Russia. Germany would then be 'encircled' and facing exactly the same situation as during the First World War.

Hitler was becoming convinced however that the Russian leader, Stalin, was suspicious of Britain and France. Stalin would have seen the way they had deserted Czechoslovakia in 1938. He may have believed that they wouldn't stand up for Poland in 1939. There were also, after all, some advantages for both Germany and Russia in making a deal, if a deal could be arranged.

On Russia's side, Stalin needed time for Russia to prepare for a future war. Then, if war did come between Britain/France and Germany, that might weaken Germany sufficiently to help Russia win later. Then, after all, Hitler was also holding out the bribe of half of Poland for nothing.

From Germany's point of view, although a war against Communist Russia was assured, *at some time in the future* (due to the opposing beliefs of the two nations), Hitler could get Poland out of the way first, then exploit the economic resources of Eastern Europe to help . him defeat France and Britain in the West, before turning on Russia.

Molotov, the new Russian Foreign minister, began to see the advantages for Russia of a deal with Nazi Germany where he could 'buy time', and the German Foreign Minister, Ribbentrop, virtually assured him that they could settle every issue from the Baltic to the Black Sea. In other words he was promising they could carve up Eastern Europe between them.

Without really any lengthy discussion (about nine days) the two sides, on 23rd August 1939, made what became known as the **Molotov-Ribbentrop Pact** (a Nazi-Soviet Non-Aggression Pact). They agreed not to attack each other, not to support anyone who attacked the other, nor join any alliances against the other.

The Russians defended this treaty, a later historian wrote:

SOURCE 6.6

'The treaty with Germany was a step which USSR was forced to take in the difficult situation that had come about in the summer of 1939. The Soviet government did not deceive itself about Hitler's aims. It understood that the treaty could not bring the USSR lasting peace but only a breathing space. When it signed the treaty ... the USSR planned to use the time gained to carry through the political and military measures needed in order to ensure the country's security ...'

SOURCE 6.7 *Molotov and Ribbentrop signing the Nazi-Soviet non-aggression pact. Stalin is in the background.*

WHAT DO YOU THINK?

1. What had Russia got to gain by a deal with Germany over Poland in 1939?
2. What had Germany got to gain by a deal with Russia over Poland in 1939?
3. Explain why the Molotov–Ribbentrop Pact was such a surprise to everybody else.

Now that he had the Non-Aggression Pact with Russia, Hitler knew that he could attack Poland, when it suited him, without any risk of an immediate war with Russia. He did not wait long. On 31st August 1939, Hitler sent the following order:

SOURCE 6.8

Supreme Commander of the Armed Forces
Most Secret
<u>*Directive No. 1 for the conduct of the war.*</u>
1 *Now that the political possibilities of disposing by peaceful means of a situation on the Eastern frontier which is intolerable for Germany are exhausted, I have determined on a solution by force.*
2 *The attack on Poland is to be made in accordance with the preparations made for Case White ...*
3 *Allotment of tasks and the operational targets remain unchanged.*
   Date of attack: September 1st
   Time: 4.45 am.

At dawn, on Friday 1st September, the German airforce began to bomb Poland and the German army smashed forward. It took two more days before Britain and France joined in, but, effectively, The Second World War had begun.

THE BRITISH AND FRENCH REACTION TO THESE EVENTS

Of all the events following Munich (September 1938) it was the German occupation of the rest of Czechoslovakia on 15th March 1939 that really caused the British government to change its policy towards Germany. The Munich Agreement was supposed to save Czechoslovakia but Germany took the rest of it anyway.

Chamberlain told the House of Commons on the afternoon of 15th March;

SOURCE 6.9

'It is natural that I should bitterly regret what has happened. But do not let us be deflected from our course because of that. Let us remember that the desire of all the peoples in the world still remains fixed on hopes of peace. The aim of this government is now, as it always has been, to promote that desire and to substitute the method of discussion for the method of force in the settlement of differences.'

From this speech, one may almost be forgiven for believing that Chamberlain still thought it was 'business as usual' with the Germans, despite the overwhelming evidence that his policy of appeasing Hitler was now totally bankrupt.

But by March 1939, the idea of further giving way to Hitler was most definitely not the mood of the British people, or the rest of the Cabinet. In fact, Chamberlain, in a speech made two days later, showed that he had got more resistance in him than his House of Commons speech suggested.

He spoke to the Birmingham Conservative Association and told them:

SOURCE 6.10

'. . . while I am not prepared to let this country commit itself to new defence agreements ... yet no greater mistake could be made than to suppose that, because we believe that war is a senseless thing, this nation has so lost its courage that it will not take part to the utmost of its power in resisting a challenge if it were made.'

This was a much stiffer comment about what was going on and reflected the belief that was becoming widespread, that Britain's peace-loving nature was being taken for granted and that there was now no stopping Hitler. Britain could see either Poland being forced to make a deal with Hitler, or Hitler conquering Poland. This would mean that Germany would move into a position of domination in Eastern Europe.

WHAT DO YOU THINK?

1. Compare the views in Chamberlain's two speeches.
2. Which view best summed up the mood of the British people by March 1939?

To try and deter Germany from dominating Eastern Europe, the British government, on 31st March 1939, made the **Anglo-Polish Alliance** where the British government said that:

SOURCE 6.11

'in the event of any action which clearly threatened Polish independence ... they would feel themselves bound at once to lend the Polish government all support in their power.'

This was quite an amazing declaration; the British government *for the first time* was guaranteeing to defend an Eastern European state. Chamberlain had done all he could to get out of giving this same guarantee to Czechoslovakia in 1938 when it would have been easier to do, had a greater chance of success and would have helped a nation with a more democratic style of government. Now the British government were doing it without any agreement with France or Russia, where there would be no chance of offering Poland practical help if conflict started, and Poland, a semi-Fascist state, as the Western powers defined it was apparently far less worth defending. It was an astounding U-turn in British foreign policy. One irony was that it was Neville Chamberlain's half brother, Austen, who had been the foreign secretary negotiating the Treaty of Locarno 13 years earlier. He had announced then that, '*Germany's eastern borders are not worth the bones of one British soldier.*'! Rarely can two brothers have been involved in such a total reversal of British foreign policy in so short a time. Given Britain's inability to give any serious practical help to Poland, the principal concern of the British government for the next five months was to find out where Russia stood on the issue, since they at least could intervene in a meaningful way! Maybe Chamberlain could have done better to check with Russia first!

WHAT DO YOU THINK?

❶ Why was the Anglo-Polish pact such a strange deal for Britain to make?

❷ Account for the differences in the views of Austen and Neville Chamberlain over Eastern Europe.

From April to August, Britain and France were in negotiations with Soviet Russia to see if an alliance could be worked out. These discussions were often half-hearted, even though in June 1939, an early *Gallup poll* showed that 84% of the British population favoured making such an alliance.

The Russians seemed to be asking for additional rights of influence over other parts of Central Europe however, and the hesitation of the British government to give these was clear. The Russians thought the British were playing a double game and their view of this was expressed in *Pravda* .

SOURCE 6.12

'It seems ... that the English and the French do not want a real agreement, or one that is acceptable to the USSR. The only thing they really want is to talk about an agreement and, by making play of the obstinacy of Soviet Union, to prepare their own public opinion for making a deal with the aggressors.'

The Soviet Ambassador in France on 10th May 1939, said:

SOURCE 6.13

'Britain and France want us to be automatically involved in a war with Germany under the obligations they have accepted, without agreement with us. They reserve for themselves the right to establish the time and the range of objectives of such a conflict.'

One can't help feeling that the Russians had got a point. To their way of looking at it, Britain could declare war on Germany, to defend Poland, yet leave the Russians to do the fighting! The Russians could then envisage Britain and France making a bargain with Germany, just like they had at Munich. The Russians did not trust Britain, yet it was Chamberlain who constantly thought that it was *the Russians* who could not be trusted. It was his reluctance that helped to scupper the chances of a deal with Russia. As the historian RAC Parker put it,

SOURCE 6.14

'Chamberlain, sometimes alone, succeeded in providing a series of justifications, if not reasons, for Soviet rejection of our alliance.'

WHAT DO YOU THINK?

1. Explain why the Russians had such a problem during 1939 in coming to an agreement with Britain.
2. Study Source 6.15. In which ways does it help sum up the Russian view? (YOU work out what the occasion was, from the information given).

SOURCE 6.15 *Cartoon by Low*

WHAT, NO CHAIR FOR ME?

On 23rd August, the British government heard the staggering news of the Nazi-Soviet Non-Aggression Pact (something they had considered to be an impossibility; a Fascist-Communist agreement!). They now realised that all their attempts to woo Russia to side with Britain had failed. Whatever happened now, Britain was in it by themselves.

SOURCE 6.16 *Cartoon by Low*

THE SCUM OF THE EARTH, I BELIEVE?

THE BLOODY ASSASSIN OF THE WORKERS, I PRESUME?

WHAT DO YOU THINK?

Comment on the meaning of the above cartoon in Source 6.16.

At dawn on 1st September, German forces invaded Poland. Britain was pledged to lend military assistance, although in practical terms it could do almost nothing. How, after all, were British military forces supposed to get there? Facts like that were irrelevant; Britain was committed to go to war.

Chamberlain made a radio broadcast to the German people early in September, which remarkably echoed those words that Duff Cooper had written to him just under a year before:

SOURCE 6.17

'Hitler gave his word that he would respect the Locarno Treaty; he broke it. He gave his word that he neither wished nor intended to annex Austria; he broke it. He declared that he would not join the Czechs into the Reich; he did so. He gave his word after Munich that he had no further territorial demands in Europe; he broke it. He gave his word that he wanted no part of Poland; he broke it. He has sworn to you for years that he was the mortal enemy of Bolshevism; he is now its ally.

Can you wonder, his word is, for us, not worth the paper it is written on? ...'

SOURCE 6.18 *The British response to the invasion of Poland*

The British government took two days to think about the Polish situation, Chamberlain briefly wondered if another conference *á la* Munich would have a chance of settling the issue this time, but was forced in the end to give Germany a two hour *ultimatum* to pull out of Poland. He knew that it would be ignored and at 11.15 am on Sunday 3rd September, Chamberlain announced to the British people that, once again, they were at war with Germany. It is possibly his most famous and saddest speech:

SOURCE 6.19

'This morning the British ambassador in Berlin handed the German government a final note stating that unless we heard from them by 11 o'clock, that they were at once prepared to withdraw their troops from Poland, a state of war would exist between us ... I have to tell you now that no such undertaking has been received and that consequently this country is at war with Germany.

Now may God bless you all and may he defend the right. For it is evil things we shall be fighting against, brute force; bad faith; injustice; oppression and persecution and against them I am certain that the right will prevail.'

WHAT DO YOU THINK?

1. Why do you think Chamberlain was so sad in his speech?
2. What does the speech suggest that Chamberlain had finally realised?

QUESTION PRACTICE

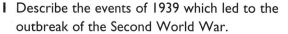

(See pages 93–99 for advice on different types of questions)

SOURCE 6.20 From a historian writing about the events leading to war in 1939

'In March 1939, Hitler broke his promise and invaded the rest of Czechoslovakia ... then he turned his attention to Poland, which had been given German land by the Treaty of Versailles. Britain now decided Hitler could not be trusted.

1 Describe the events of 1939 which led to the outbreak of the Second World War.

(Outcome 1 – 3 marks)

(Use the above source and recall)

OR

2 Why did Britain go to war with Germany in September 1939?
(Outcome 2 – 3 marks)

(Use the above source and recall)

QUESTION PRACTICE

3 Describe the events in 1939 which led to Britain declaring war on Germany in September.

(Outcome 2 – 4 marks)

SOURCE 6.21 From EH Carr's book *International relations between the two world wars*

'The immediate dispute concerned Germany's demand for the return of Danzig and the so-called corridor, which had been separated from Germany by the Versailles Treaty. The Poles

refused to give way and Germany started an invasion of Poland. This took place on September 1st. On September 3rd, war was declared by Britain.'

4 Why did the Second World War start in September 1939?

(Outcome 2 – 4 marks)

(Use the source and recall)

7

THE BRITISH RESPONSE: THE POLICY OF APPEASEMENT

This chapter will do four things:
- ◆ look at some possible definitions of appeasement
- ◆ look at the background to the policy of appeasement before Chamberlain
- ◆ look at the wider picture of the international and domestic circumstances in which the British government was operating in the 1930s
- ◆ come to conclusions on the different ways the policy can be viewed.

INTRODUCTION

Historians and students have often been critical of the conduct of British foreign policy during the 1930s. They accuse Chamberlain of following a failed policy which achieved nothing. It looked cringing and cowardly even as it was being operated and it brought Britain humiliation and shame.

In March 1938, Churchill had made this point in a speech in the House of Commons:

SOURCE 7.1

'… historians a thousand years from now will still be baffled by the mystery of our affairs. They will never understand how it was that a victorious nation, with everything in hand, let themselves be brought low, to cast away all that they had gained … gone with the wind. Britain were the victors but are now defeated, and Germany, who threw down their arms in the field and sued for armistice are striding on to world mastery.'

Churchill was asking how it could be explained that Britain could have been so great and so much in charge, and yet the policies of the British government had somehow let Germany get back on top. This view was also put forward in a famous article by 'Cato' in 1940 that suggested that Chamberlain's government were 'The Guilty Men' who didn't have the guts to stand up to Hitler, and therefore helped to bring about the Second World War. These claims raise a lot of serious questions; how valid is this 'Guilty Men' view? Is there any defence of Chamberlain? Could another Prime Minister really have behaved differently?

SOME POSSIBLE DEFINITIONS OF APPEASEMENT

Historians writing on this topic have their own definitions of what appeasement means. Each have their own way of putting it so that extra meaning is added, depending on whether they want it to sound apologetic or whether they want to imply shame and guilt! Appeasement has therefore become a 'value-laden' word; how you use it gives it meaning!

Collins Dictionary definition of appeasement is: '*An act of pacifying ... making substantial concessions to preserve peace'* but that is rather a bland view. It doesn't really fit with Chamberlain's own definition that appeasement was ...

SOURCE 7.2

'... by the exercise of friendliness, and understanding of what were the desires of others ... to clear up all differences by discussion, without armed conflict ...'

Chamberlain's view seems to miss out the notion that anything is given away!

The historian Martin Gilbert backs Chamberlain up by saying:

SOURCE 7.3

'Appeasement was not a silly or treacherous idea, it was not held by stubborn or simple men – it was a noble idea. It was rooted in Christianity, in courage and common sense.'

But that brave defence of appeasement doesn't really square with the view of T.P. Cuthbert that appeasement was nothing more than:

SOURCE 7.4

'The soothing of threatening enemies by giving way to their demands.'

This seems a much more honest and critical view of what appeasement actually was in practice; a view supported by Dr E. Ranson's cutting statement that appeasement was:

SOURCE 7.5

'A policy where you buy off your enemies by selling your friends.'

These different views are somewhat pulled together in Professor William Rock's summary that appeasement was:

SOURCE 7.6

'A policy of identifying the basic grievances of your enemies and attempting to remove them through reasonable negotiation.'

None of the historians seem to have come up with any idea of what Hitler's view of the policy of appeasement was! The closest we possibly get was when he was asked what he thought of British statesmen and he said *'I have seen them, they are like worms.'*

Any students of British foreign policy over the 1930s will therefore come to their own view as to which definition of appeasement best fits with their interpretation of the events of that decade. Be aware that the word appeasement can be a word of honour or a word of shame, depending how you use it.

WHAT DO YOU THINK?

❶ Why do historians have to be very careful about how they use the word appeasement?

❷ If you were a *supporter* of the policy of appeasement, what qualities would you say it possessed?

❸ If you were a *critic* of the policy of appeasement, what features of it would you stress?

THE BACKGROUND TO THE POLICY OF APPEASEMENT BEFORE CHAMBERLAIN

It seems easy to criticise Chamberlain as the peddler of a failed policy from 1937 onwards, since he seemed to so *personalise* the way the diplomacy was conducted. He was right there himself with his 'shuttle diplomacy', travelling round Europe, being filmed getting on and off planes and giving his 'sound-bite' statements to the newsreel cameras. No wonder that the tendency is to heap the criticism on him when it all failed in September 1939, as if he alone was to blame. However, apart from his personal intervention, was he doing anything new or different from what British foreign ministers and statesmen before him might have done? The answer is probably not. Part of the defence of Chamberlain's actions therefore lies in the fact that with his policy of appeasement he was largely continuing a traditional British foreign policy; it was not something totally new that Chamberlain had concocted himself.

A closer look at British foreign policy actions since 1919 concerning Europe shows that just about every one of them has some aspect of appeasement in them. Almost all Britain's moments of major European diplomacy seemed somehow to be tied into revising the operation of the terms of the Treaty of Versailles. The British government and people had come more and more to believe that they had been wrong in going for the 'revenge' policy at Versailles and were therefore prepared to rectify that mistake. In its most favourable light this was what appeasement was. It was not seen as a humiliating climb-down, but as a thoughtful and honourable attempt to restore good relations by compromise. This is shown by the following:

- **Locarno Pact 1925** – Britain accepted the re-negotiation of some of the terms of Versailles in a spirit of co-operation
- **Ending of reparations 1932** – Britain accepted that the demands on Germany were too great and cancelled the debt
- **Geneva Disarmament Conference 1932–33** – Britain supported the idea of letting Germany have controlled re-armament
- **Work for peace within the Covenant of the League of Nations** – Britain stuck by the League of Nations as a peace keeper (up to Abyssinian Crisis 1935)
- **Anglo-German Naval Deal 1935** – Britain accepted that Germany was going to do it anyway
- **Hoare-Laval Pact over Abyssinian Crisis 1935** – Britain accepted that Mussolini could not be stopped, and tried to do a deal over Abyssinia to save going to war
- **Rhineland 1936** – Britain accepted that Germany had a case and would not support France in any military action

When one considers this catalogue of appeasing actions, it is clearly possible to see Chamberlain's actions from 1937–39 as a natural part of this overall policy of giving 'concessions'.

WHAT DO YOU THINK?

1 Why is it easy to make *personal* criticism of Chamberlain when one is criticising appeasement?
2 What evidence could be put forward to suggest that the policy of appeasement was Britain's *traditional* European foreign policy of the 1920s and 1930s?

Another major defence of Chamberlain lies in the fact that he was forced to operate within a wider framework of domestic and international circumstances, which had a great influence on his freedom of action. In other words, he was almost forced to behave the way he did because of the effect of all these *constraints*. In the 1960s and 70s, there were more historians who looked at it from this point of view and were prepared to defend Chamberlain and his policies. They were known as '*revisionists*' because they were revising the existing views which were so critical of him. These historians argued that the 'Guilty Men' approach was flawed because it didn't allow consideration of the wider factors that Chamberlain had to take into account.

THE WIDER PICTURE OF THE INTERNATIONAL AND DOMESTIC CIRCUMSTANCES IN WHICH THE BRITISH GOVERNMENT WAS OPERATING IN THE 1930s

There were a whole range of factors which influenced the way Chamberlain's government behaved in conducting its foreign policy. These factors varied in their influence, they were not all important all the time, nor were they all as important as each other. They are not listed in order of importance, but they all help answer the question '**WHY** *did Chamberlain follow the policy of appeasement?*'

HATRED OF WAR

Chamberlain was not alone in Britain in hating the idea of another war as dreadful as the Great War had been. To him, it was worth doing almost anything to avoid a war.

Chamberlain's personal view of war is best summed up in a moving speech he gave in 1938:

SOURCE 7.7

'When I think of those four terrible years and I think of the seven million young men who were cut off in their prime, the 13 million who were maimed and mutilated, the misery and suffering of the mothers and fathers and friends of those who were killed and wounded ... now I am bound to say. ... In war, whichever side calls itself the victor, there are no winners, but all are losers ... It is those thoughts which have made me feel that it was my prime duty to strain every nerve to avoid repetition of the Great War in Europe.'

Chamberlain believed that most of the British population supported him in these feelings. In the early 1930s, the Oxford University Union debate that *'This House will in no circumstances fight for King and Country'* and the 1935 Peace Ballot, had both seemed to give evidence of the widespread *pacifist* attitudes of the British people at that time. Chamberlain did not think the British people were any more willing to go to war by the later 1930s.

In fact, the later 1930s seemed to provide evidence of even greater possibilities of devastation if a new war broke out. Chamberlain was horrified about the possible effects that a widespread bombing campaign could have on *civilian* populations. In April 1937, the Spanish town of Guernica was destroyed in an afternoon by German bombers during the Spanish Civil War. Chamberlain believed the same could happen to London: that there could be as many as 600 000 deaths in the first six months of war. He shared the commonly held view of the time that 'The bomber will always get through'.

However, Chamberlain tended to overlook the following:
- The effects of bombing an un-warned, defenceless Spanish market town may not have been the same as those on a British city that had been warned (by radar), prepared (by the ARP) and defended (by fighter aircraft).
- The tendency to over-estimate the threat of the German bomber. The size of the *Luftwaffe* was not as big as some sources seemed to indicate and therefore the damage that German bombers could cause may not have actually been as great as he thought.
- Neither the British nor the Germans had a long range bomber capable of flying to each other's countries (and back!) in the 1930s, therefore, in the short run, he shouldn't have been as worried as he often dramatically made out.

WHAT DO YOU THINK?

1. What evidence supported Chamberlain in his view that the British people hated war and therefore it should be avoided at all costs?
2. What factors suggest that Chamberlain may have been misled about the effects of aerial war on Britain?

BRITISH MILITARY READINESS

Any Prime minister has to take advice from his 'experts'. In the case of military matters, Chamberlain consulted **CIGS** (The Chiefs of the Imperial General Staff). They generally tended to give pessimistic advice, which Chamberlain had to accept, since he could hardly know better than they did. CIGS told him in December 1937:

SOURCE 7.8

'... our Naval, Military and Air Forces, in their present stage of development, are still not enough to meet our defensive commitments which now extend from Western Europe, through the Mediterranean to the Far East. We cannot see the time when our defence forces will be strong enough to safeguard our territory, trade and vital interests against Germany, Italy and Japan simultaneously. It is important therefore to do anything that will reduce the numbers of our potential enemies and to gain the support of possible allies.'

Generally, their advice agreed with what Chamberlain wanted to hear and could therefore be used to support his arguments in Parliament. Chamberlain knew that in public at least he had to speak up *against* re-armament, since the British public appeared so peace-loving. Historians generally believe that Chamberlain wasn't totally in favour of this disarmament policy. He may have been an appeaser, but more than anyone else, he wanted to see Britain with a strong military force that could stand up for itself.

The historian D.C. Watt wrote:

SOURCE 7.9

'He had been at the centre of British re-armament efforts since it started in 1934 and had pressed it forward ...'

In 1937, Chamberlain himself said:

SOURCE 7.10

'I believe the double policy of re-armament and better relations with Germany and Italy, will carry us safely through the danger period.'

The other factor limiting Chamberlain's ambitions to re-arm was the attitude of the British Treasury, saying it would cost too much. In the later 1930s Britain was still climbing out of the economic slump of the Great Depression. Governments had a choice to spend their limited money on either 'Welfare or Warfare'. The Treasury told Chamberlain he could not have both, and that the available money was better spent on the British people than preparing for war.

WHAT DO YOU THINK?

1 In which ways did CIGS influence Chamberlain into following a policy of appeasement?
2 In which ways did the British Treasury influence Chamberlain into following a policy of appeasement?
3 In his re-armament policy, was Chamberlain as much a coward as some have made out?

SYMPATHY WITH GERMANY, AND NO BRITISH INTERESTS AT STAKE IN EASTERN EUROPE

We have already seen, as we have looked at the different diplomatic incidents of the 1930s, that there was a fair degree of sympathy in Britain for Germany's position. It was felt that Germany had been persecuted by the terms of the Treaty of Versailles and had a 'just' cause for complaint. Nevile Henderson, the British ambassador in Berlin wrote:

SOURCE 7.11

'I believed there was no real possibility of stability either in Germany or Europe generally, until the grievances arising out of Versailles ... which had created Hitler, had been corrected.'

Besides being prepared to let the Germans revise the terms of Versailles relating to Western Europe, the British government also tended to have a 'do-a-deal mentality' over Germany's behaviour in Eastern Europe. Chamberlain was not alone in thinking that Eastern Europe was not Britain's business; the general view was that the Germans should be allowed to manage what was 'theirs' in return for letting Britain manage its own business.

The Sunday Times on 31st March 1935 noted that:

SOURCE 7.12

'... Our country has no real interest in Eastern Europe, has no intention of taking an active part in defending a peace settlement in which she has ceased to believe.'

Chamberlain summed up his own view that Eastern Europe was not Britain's business in his somewhat insensitive speech of 27th September 1938, referring to Czechoslovakia as *'that far away country of which we know little'*. This view that Eastern Europe was no concern of Britain's came to grief by the time of Germany's invasion of Poland in September 1939, when it was realised that there wasn't a territorial limit to what Germany considered as 'theirs'.

WHAT DO YOU THINK?

1 What was Britain's attitude towards Germany and the terms of the Treaty of Versailles in Western Europe?

2 What was Britain's attitude towards Germany and the terms of the Treaty of Versailles in Eastern Europe?

FRENCH WEAKNESS

Tied in with Britain's sympathy towards Germany, was a growing exasperation with the attitudes and position of Britain's old ally, France. Increasingly over the 1930s the British came to see that France was weak and unstable internally, unreliable as an ally, and their reluctance to compromise was more the cause of European friction than Germany herself.

France did face problems electing a strong government of any great staying power; leading to the joke of the time that *'American tourists went to London to see the changing of the guard and then to Paris to see the changing of the government'*.

Chamberlain didn't really like or trust the French. He said of the French that they:

SOURCE 7.13

'... can never keep a secret for more than half an hour or a government for more than nine months.'

The British government had seen the weakness and hesitancy of France's 'Maginot mentality' at work during the 1936 Rhineland Crisis, and generally, the French seemed to look to Britain for a lead before they would ever do anything. Chamberlain was worried that if he gave them too much support, they might become too aggressive towards Germany, so his room for manoeuvre in diplomacy must have been limited by this worry over how much he could rely on France.

WHAT DO YOU THINK?

In which ways did a distrust of France cause Britain to follow a policy of appeasement?

IMPERIAL COMMITMENTS AND THE INFLUENCE OF THE BRITISH COMMONWEALTH

Although Britain was coming to appreciate she was no longer a major great power, she still had both an Empire (in India, SE Asia, large parts of Africa, the Caribbean and Pacific islands) and a Commonwealth (largely the white dominions of Canada,

Australia/New Zealand and South Africa) to lead and protect. Their defence was a priority and that meant avoiding getting into any precarious positions of defending other states in Europe. The British government knew that its naval power was spread very thinly round the globe. It would be difficult to find enough naval forces to fight in both the Mediterranean and the Far East. Had Britain really got enough ships to defend its Pacific possessions and Australia if Japan became aggressive? In these circumstances, the British government felt its best option might be to try and stay out of European involvements.

Then what about the Commonwealth's involvement in any future war? Britain was well aware of the debt it owed to Commonwealth forces in the First World War. As Britain's power had waned, troops from the Commonwealth had increasingly come to the battlefield and carried the strain. They had believed then that they were doing it as their duty to the Motherland. Would they do it again? Could Britain seriously ask its Commonwealth allies to come and bail Britain out if it got involved in a war over Czechoslovakia? After all, why on earth should they regard it as any business of theirs? To some extent Britain already had the answer. South Africa had indicated that it would not help, Australia and New Zealand wouldn't commit themselves, while only Canada said 'Yes'.

WHAT DO YOU THINK?

How were Britain's worries about its Empire different from its worries about its Commonwealth?

NON-INTERVENTION OF USA

Like the Commonwealth nations, America had, eventually, participated in the First World War and contributed towards the ultimate victory of the allies. Would it be possible to rely on them again?

The clear signal right through the 1920s was that America had become 'isolationist' and wanted nothing more to do with Europe's petty quarrels. The refusal of the United States Congress to agree to join the League of Nations in 1920 was a sign of them turning their backs on involvement in Western Europe. Then, the **Neutrality Acts** of 1935 and 1937 reinforced the message that they didn't feel that European problems were their business.

It is possible that America may have been more interested in defending European democracies than Britain realised, and it has been claimed that the somewhat pro-German American ambassador in Britain, Joe Kennedy, gave a rather misleading message about America's position. He implied that Britain *had* to do a deal with Germany because it could *not* rely *at all* on American assistance. The American position may not have been as simple as this and Chamberlain may have had more support from President Roosevelt than he realised. America did, after all, come into the Second World War on Britain's side in 1941, but Chamberlain was not to know that in 1938.

In 1933 Chamberlain had written that when it came to the United States:

SOURCE 7.14

'We have the misfortune to be dealing with a nation of cads.'

This comment seems to bracket Americans in with the French as people that Chamberlain felt he could not depend on for support in his policy of appeasement! However the claim that Chamberlain ignored the possibility of American help because he didn't like them is now generally being shown by historians to have been misjudged. There is more evidence that by 1937, Chamberlain was capable of realistically considering any offer the Americans might make, but felt they couldn't be relied on to step in to help.

This view was summed up in Chamberlain's classic comment that

SOURCE 7.15

'It was always best and safest to count on nothing from the Americans except words.'

DISTRUST OF RUSSIA

For a variety of reasons, the option of trying to make an agreement with Russia was ignored by Chamberlain.

◆ Like all Conservatives, he was fearful of the spread of Communism. It was said of Britain's ruling class that whereas they hated Bolshevism, they only disliked Fascism! Chamberlain himself said:

SOURCE 7.16

'I must confess to a most profound distrust of Russia ... I distrust her motives, which seem to me to have little connection with our ideas of liberty ...'

◆ Chamberlain wasn't convinced that the Russians were strong enough to do anything. Stalin had purged the Russian Red Army in 1937–38, executing tens of thousands of its officers. British intelligence over-estimated the effect this had on the fighting capacity of the Red Army. It was thought that it would take years for Russia to recover its military strength, and, in the meantime, it could not help effectively by intervening in any European events.
◆ Chamberlain also believed that there was great danger in making an alliance with Russia and re-creating what looked like the old pre-1914 Triple Entente. This would just make Germany feel trapped and 'encircled' and therefore even more dangerous and less likely to back down.

Chamberlain told the House of Commons:

SOURCE 7.17

'We set our faces against dividing Europe into opposing blocks of powers, joined together into alliances. That system has gone and is not likely to be revived.'

WHAT DO YOU THINK?

① What factors influenced Chamberlain's approach to bringing the Americans into participating in his policy of appeasement?

② What factors influenced Chamberlain's approach to bringing the Russians into participating in his policy of appeasement?

THE POLITICAL INNOCENCE OF BRITAIN'S LEADERS

There is a case for saying that the British government followed a policy of appeasement because they just did not know any better. In other words, in the face of everything telling them it was a crazy policy just to keep giving way to Hitler, Chamberlain was locked into that way of looking at things. He just could not believe that it would not, in the end, work.

We have already referred to Chamberlain's strictly conventional, honourable, 'play-the-game' approach to diplomacy. He had got a business background before going into politics, and in both areas, he was used to doing deals with men he felt he could trust. This tended to give him a limited point of view and certainly did not give him the experience needed to deal with Hitler. This new problem for Chamberlain was summed up nicely by a British diplomat who said:

SOURCE 7.18

'The trouble with conducting diplomacy in the 1930s was that you didn't know if you were dealing with clever men who were bluffing or maniacs who really meant it.'

The fact, however, that others *at the time* noticed this problem, means that Chamberlain should not be too readily excused. Duff Cooper thought that Chamberlain's policy of appeasement was little more than wishful thinking and said so. He cuttingly commented that Chamberlain had as much chance of appeasing Hitler as:

SOURCE 7.19

'Little Lord Fauntleroy would have of concluding a satisfactory deal with Al Capone.'

WHAT DO YOU THINK?

What evidence supports a view that Chamberlain's attitudes made him unsuited to pursuing a policy of appeasement with someone like Hitler?

CONCLUSIONS ON THE DIFFERENT INTERPRETATIONS OF THE POLICY OF APPEASEMENT

There is no easy conclusion regarding the policy of appeasement and how Britain, under Chamberlain, chose to operate it in the later 1930s. Historians themselves seem to go through 'fashions' of either defending Chamberlain or criticising him.

In the 1940s and 1950s there was strong criticism of the policy, which had so clearly failed. The fact that it had been pursued, on Britain's behalf, by a rather prim and pathetic 70 year old, who was out-manoeuvred at every turn, just seemed to sum up the idiocy of the whole idea. Chamberlain looked like a 'loser' who had let Britain stumble into a second great war. He was the 'Guilty Man'.

By the 1960s and 1970s however, the '*revisionist*' historians were more prepared to look at the *circumstances* within which Chamberlain had to operate. They feel his policy of negotiation and concession should not be so simply criticised since it was the 'British way'. They also argue that Chamberlain was not as simple as he looked, and that by delaying British entry into war he had given Britain a greater chance to re-arm. It can easily be argued, after all, that the greatest blame for the war lies at the feet of Hitler and his ambitions rather than the mistakes of Chamberlain. Historians supporting Chamberlain therefore argue that he had little room for manoeuvre due to all the limits placed on him by other factors, and that really he did the best he could in the circumstances.

In a radio speech to the British people in September 1939, at the outbreak of war, he made this very point:

SOURCE 7.20

'You can imagine what a bitter blow it is to me that all my long struggle to win peace has failed. Yet I cannot believe that there is anything more or anything different that I could have done that would have been more successful.'

This rather complacent view (that he had no choices) would not have the support of the most modern school of historians studying Chamberlain's policies. Over the 1980s and 1990s the 'post-revisionist' view has developed. They agree that Chamberlain *was* severely limited by the circumstances within which he had to operate, but nevertheless he was able to make choices about policy which could have led to things turning out differently. They argue that due to Chamberlain's arrogance, he either made predictable choices or wrong ones. And from among these wrong choices the greatest one was linked to Chamberlain's attitude towards Russia.

So, this area of debate is by no means over. There are still plenty of historians around to defend or criticise Chamberlain (or other statesmen from the time like Halifax, Henderson or Churchill), or look for new explanations of factors that helped influence British foreign policy.

The fact that, of all the European and World topics on the Intermediate and Higher syllabus, the *Appeasement and the Road to War* topic has *by far* the largest number of pupils studying it, is a witness to the enduring interest and relevance that this area still has to our understanding of the nature of the diplomacy of power politics. The legacy of Britain's behaviour concerning events more than 60 years ago is still with us; an example for us to learn from. Chamberlain's doubts and certainties, his hopes and failures, the shame and drama are all there as an early model for any aspiring student of the enduring problems of international peacemaking.

Perhaps the last word on this should be left with Winston Churchill. Given his years of resistance to Chamberlain's policies, and the knowledge by 1940 that he had been proven right by events, you may have thought that he was not the most suitable person to give an address following Chamberlain's funeral. Yet the charitable and sensitive words that Churchill spoke to the House of Commons on 12th November 1940, in many ways summed up the whole policy of appeasement:

SOURCE 7.21

'It fell to Neville Chamberlain in one of the supreme crises of the world to be contradicted by events, to be disappointed in his hopes and to be deceived and cheated by a wicked man'.

SOURCE 7.22

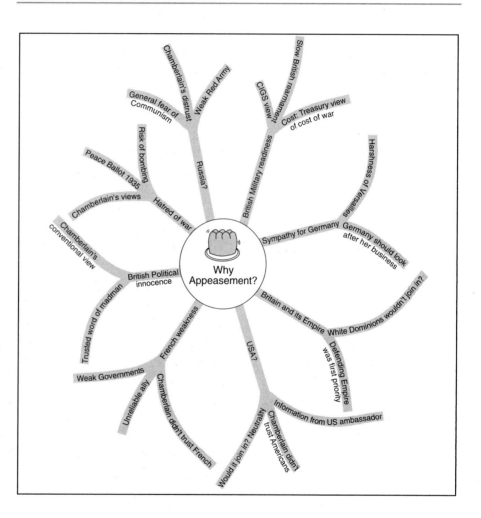

QUESTION PRACTICE

(See pages 93–99 for advice on different types of questions)

SOURCE 7.23 From Andrew Boxer's *Appeasement*

The losses of the First World War were enormous and created a widespread feeling that death on such a scale should never be allowed to happen again. Then there were constant arguments between Britain's military chiefs about how to best use Britain's limited military resources to defend the United Kingdom and her Empire.

1 Why did Chamberlain feel that Britain must follow a policy of appeasement towards Hitler?

(Outcome 2 – 4 marks)

(Use the source and recalled knowledge).

SOURCE 7.24 From an editorial in the *Aberdeen Press and Journal* October 1938

'No-one who lived through the 1914–18 struggle, whether facing imminent death in the trenches or in the nerve-wracked atmosphere at home, could contemplate another war. For lives of suffering spared and for horrors averted, Europe's thanks are due to Mr Chamberlain'.

2 How useful is this source in explaining the reasons why Chamberlain pursued a policy of appeasement in the later 1930s?

(Outcome 3 – 4 marks)

(Use the source and recalled knowledge)

QUESTION PRACTICE

SOURCE 7.25 From the memoirs of Lord Halifax, the Foreign Secretary 1938–1940

'Once the Austrian Anschluss had taken place, it was no longer possible to defend Czechoslovakia. When all has been said, one fact cannot be challenged. When war did come, a year after Munich, it found a country and Commonwealth totally united and prepared. They were also convinced that every effort had been made to avoid war. And that was the big thing Chamberlain did'.

3 How useful is this source in justifying the British policy of appeasement in the late 1930s? *(Outcome 3 – 4 marks)*

4 Why was there support in Britain in the 1930s for the government's policy of appeasement? *(Outcome 2 – 5 marks)*

There is also the possibility of an 8-mark short essay

What were the main reasons for Britain's appeasement of Germany from 1933 to 1939? *(Outcomes 1 and 2 – 8 marks)*

8 SECOND WORLD WAR: WHERE DID RESPONSIBILITY LIE?

FROM BRITAIN'S POINT OF VIEW

It is easy to argue that Britain did all it could to avoid going to war. The operation of Chamberlain's policy of appeasement is evidence for that. Indeed, the longer Chamberlain carried on appeasing Hitler, the more likely it was that war could indeed be avoided. *But* the British government finally drew the line in the sand at Poland and said that Hitler had gone far enough. Britain's behaviour was always honourable, Hitler was sent a final clear signal over Poland, but he ignored it. It seems Britain is therefore cleared of any blame for bringing about the start of the Second World War.

But did Britain really mean it or was the Polish pact a bluff, designed to frighten Hitler rather than defend Poland? After all, did Hitler really expect Britain to stand up for Poland in 1939 when it had not stood up for anyone else before that? Surely all the evidence was that Britain would do a deal as usual? The historian William Carr refers to Hitler actually being *'badly shaken'* in August 1939, by the news that Britain *would* stand by Poland.

However, Britain's sense of determination had begun to emerge a little earlier than that, and maybe Hitler misread it. By March 1939 both the British government and the British people had come to realise that Hitler was unreasonable and could neither be trusted nor negotiated with. The Czech Crisis had helped cause a change of mood where it was felt that Hitler has been given his last chance. Up until then, Britain had been sympathetic to his claims of revising Versailles and retrieving 'lost Germans' but the view of him now was that unless someone did something soon, this was a man who could not be stopped. He was wanting to entirely destroy Versailles and redraw the map of Europe. This change of view had led to a fairly rapid acceleration of Britain's re-armament, including the unprecedented step of introducing peacetime conscription into the British army in April 1939. These things should have convinced Hitler that Britain now meant business, but it is difficult to be sure.

FROM GERMANY'S POINT OF VIEW

Historians have spent much time (especially in the 1960s and 1970s) arguing over whether Hitler had a plan which inevitably led to war. The reason why this debate mattered was that if it could be proved that there *was* a plan, then clearly nothing Chamberlain could have done would have made any difference. Therefore Chamberlain would become cleared of any blame for causing the war by his policy of appeasement, and the whole responsibility would rest with Germany.

If, on the other hand, it could be proved that Hitler had no plan, then the case *against* Chamberlain would look stronger. It could then be argued that the war was caused, partly at least, by the muddled and blundering path followed by Chamberlain in trying to do a deal with Hitler.

Those who supported the view that there **was** a plan (known as the 'programme school') used the evidence of the 1920 Nazi 25 Point Programme, Hitler's writings in *Mein Kampf* and especially the Hossbach Memorandum 1937. The historian Hugh Trevor Roper argued that:

SOURCE 8.1

'Hitler's war aims were written large and clear in the documents of his reign.'

Those historians who argued against the idea of Hitler having a plan referred to problems in using/interpreting all that evidence, and Hitler's own personality and style which preferred flexibility of action to fixed ideas.

This debate seems to have rather fizzled out in the past 15 years into a sort of compromise view: that Hitler did have a broader strategic view (Hitler's *'wish list'*!) but he hadn't laid down any precise means of achieving it. Therefore, war *was* an option but it wasn't written into the script to start the Second World War on the 1st September 1939. This view sees Hitler as an opportunist who was always on the look out for (or to cause) a set of unsettled international circumstances which favoured a bit of nifty 'statecraft' where Hitler could see what he could gain. It may be that by 1939 and Poland, Hitler believed he had got the measure of all his diplomatic opponents and over-reached himself through conceit, but that isn't the same as saying that he planned to start the Second World War over it

So, no serious historian would claim that Britain was responsible for causing the outbreak of the Second World War; the issue really is the degree of responsibility that can be placed on Germany. Was it the whim of a madman determined on world domination, a series of diplomatic manoeuvres that got out of hand, arrogance in misreading a situation or was it insanity? The evidence supports so many different shades of opinion that these questions are impossible to answer in simple terms, and that only adds to the intrigue created by this whole period of history.

TEST AND EXAM ADVICE

There are three basic types of question (outcomes). They are listed below together with a description of what you must do for each (performance criteria or PCs). *Parts in italics are only needed for Intermediate 2.* The length of answers will depend on the number of marks. Try to include at least one developed point for each mark.

Outcome 1.

Description questions which ask you to show your knowledge and understanding of historical developments, events and issues.

a) you must use recalled knowledge which is relevant to the question; at Intermediate 1 you must also use relevant information from the source(s).

b) your knowledge from recall (and the source(s) at Intermediate 1) must show accurate understanding of the topic and its themes and issues.

Outcome 2.

Explanation questions which ask you to explain historical developments and events. You usually have to explain the reasons for, or the results of something.

a) Int. 1 – your explanation must be supported by accurate information from recall and the source(s).
Int. 2 – your explanation must be supported by relevant information from recall and the source(s).

b) Int. 1 – your explanation must be supported by relevant information from recall and the source(s).
Int. 2 – your explanation must use accurate information.

c) *Int. 2 only – your answer must have an introduction and conclusion (this relates mainly to the 8-mark short essay question – see page 94).*

Outcome 3.

Source evaluation questions which ask you to evaluate historical sources with reference to their context (what was happening at the time). These usually ask you how useful, reliable or accurate a source is.

a) Int. 1 – your evaluation must take into account the origin or purpose of the source (who wrote it? when was it written? why was it written? etc.).

Int. 2 – you must also take into account the context of the source(s (relevant information about what was happening at the time).

b) Int. 1 – your evaluation must show you understand what is in the source.

Int 2 – your evaluation must take into account the content of the source. You can also point out what the source fails to mention.

c) *Int. 2 only – you must be able to make an accurate comparison between two sources.*

HOW TO WRITE YOUR 8 MARK ESSAY.

One of the questions in internal tests and the final exam at Intermediate 2 is the 8-mark essay question.

It is an explanation type of question for which you usually have to explain the reasons for or results of something.

Remember that your essay

◆ must have an introduction
◆ must have a middle section with paragraphs for each of your main points
◆ must have a separate conclusion.

Making a Plan

It often helps to jot down a list of about five main points you want to deal with before you start your essay. You can add to the list if more points occur to you.

Introduction: This is worth 1 or 2 marks.

It should deal with the question. It might only be a sentence or two. You could start with a sentence like this: *'There were many reasons why ... (such and such happened). These reasons were ...'*

Middle section. This is worth 5 marks.

If you have five main points you should have five paragraphs in the middle section of your essay.

Each paragraph should start with a sentence which sets out what the paragraph will be about. You should then explain what your main point means or how it is connected to the question.

You then go on to use accurate and relevant facts to explain what you mean and show off what you know.

Conclusion. This is worth 1 or 2 marks.

It should be a paragraph of a few sentences.

It should sum up your answer. It could be something like this – *'In conclusion, there were lots of reasons why ... (such and such happened) These reasons included ...(sum up your main points).'*

In your conclusion you should:
◆ sum up the points you have explained earlier in the answer. You could also say which points you think were the most important and give reasons

◆ make up your mind and answer the question that you were asked.

Use this pattern in future 8-mark short essay answers. You can also use it to help you with your extended response. Remember you only have to do one 8-mark essay in the exam. Use the advice in this section to help you get it right.

The following example shows how an 8-mark essay can be organised. The question is: *What were the main reasons for Germany's aggressive foreign policy in the 1930s?*

Introduction

'There are several reasons which help to explain why Germany had such an aggressive foreign policy in the 1930s. These reasons were....'
(You might include opposition to the Treaty of Versailles, [3 or 4 separate factors could be included in this], Hitler's policy of *Lebensraum* and Hitler's beliefs in German superiority, as three key areas.)

Middle section

This will have three parts (large paragraphs) in it where you give the important historical information which helps answer the question. Your first paragraph could start like this ...
'The first reason why German foreign policy was so aggressive was Hitler's determination to revise the terms of Versailles. Severe restrictions had been placed on Germany over what weapons she could have....'
You continue with whatever information you know about Hitler's plans to revise Versailles to make Germany more powerful.

Your next paragraph could follow the same pattern:
'The second reason for Germany's aggressive foreign policy can be seen in the beliefs of the Nazi Party about Lebensraum. Hitler and the Nazis believed that Germany did not have enough space for its growing population....'
You continue with whatever information you know about Hitler's plans to advance eastwards to get more 'living space'.

You would then have your third big paragraph with information on Hitler's views about Germans being the master race.

Conclusion

Your Conclusion should sum up your answer. It could be something like this ...
'There were three main reasons why Germany's foreign policy was so aggressive during the 1930s. They were all to do with the policies that Hitler introduced after he came to power in 1933. Hitler's determination to make Germany strong again meant that he constantly tried to change the terms of the Treaty of Versailles. He also thought that Germans were better than every other race and should try and conquer them, and he believed that Germany needed spare land for its extra population to spread into. These factors help

to explain why German foreign policy was so aggressive towards other countries in the 1930s.'

In your conclusion you have:

1 referred to the main question,
2 shown that you know several reasons that explain Germany's aggressive foreign policy,
3 summed up the points you made in the middle section.

This sort of pattern needs to be followed whenever you do an 8-mark short essay question.

EXTENDED RESPONSE ADVICE

Intermediate 2 candidates must also produce a longer prepared essay as part of the external course assessment – usually round about February/March.

This is called the Extended Response and is worth one quarter of the final marks. It is similar to the 8-mark short essay (see page 94). The main differences are:

◆ It will be much longer than an 8-mark short essay. You will have an hour to write it. It could be up to 1000 words long (four or five sides of A4).
◆ You choose your own question relating to one of the three units making up your course. Your teacher can advise you on this.
◆ You research and prepare your answer by reading and taking notes from a variety of sources. Your teacher can help you with sources.
◆ You prepare a plan of 150 words with sub-headings which you can take into the final writing-up session. Your teacher can check your plan for you.
◆ A teacher will supervise the final one-hour writing-up session under exam conditions, but cannot help you in any way. Your plan and response are then sent to the SQA for marking.

CHOOSING A QUESTION

◆ Pick a topic that interests you and that you feel you can do well in.
◆ Discuss the exact wording of the question with your teacher.
◆ Choose a question that requires you to explain and assess what happened rather than simply describing events.
◆ Avoid questions which cover too much or which are too vague or too narrow.
◆ You should be able to divide it up into about five sub-headings.
◆ Some possible questions from this unit are given on the next page.

READING AND NOTE-TAKING

Talk to your teacher about sources.
As you read, jot down notes for your different sub-headings

(either using separate sheets for each sub-heading or by indicating in the margin which sub-heading each note is about).

Use key words and avoid copying whole sentences and paragraphs – try to use one or two good short 'quotes'.

PREPARING YOUR PLAN

Use your notes to prepare your 150 word plan.

This should consist of sub-headings and key points to remind you of what you want to include.

There is an example of a plan on page 99.

You could also draw a spider diagram like this to help you:

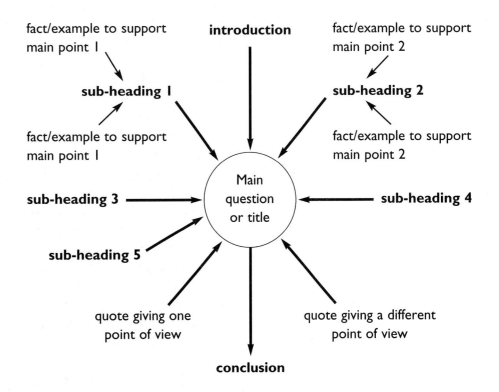

If you want, you can write a practise draft of your full response, but you cannot take it into the final write-up session with you.

You are only allowed to take in your plan of **not more than 150 words**.

THE WRITE-UP SESSION

Your plan will enable you to work your way steadily through your response.

You have one hour to do this, allowing about ten minutes for each sub-heading and leaving time for your conclusion.

Try to concentrate on explanation and analysis rather than just description and narrative.

If you are running out of time, make quick notes about any remaining sub-heading(s) and go straight to your conclusion.

POSSIBLE EXTENDED RESPONSE QUESTIONS

◆ What were the main factors influencing Hitler's foreign policy between 1933 and 1939?

◆ What were the main reasons for Germany's aggressive foreign policy in the 1930s?

◆ Do you agree that revision of the Treaty of Versailles was the most significant part of Hitler's foreign policy?

◆ *'Hitler's foreign policy was nothing but Racism and Revisionism.'* Do you agree?

◆ Why was Hitler able to get away with the re-occupation of the Rhineland in March 1936?

◆ How important were British and French attitudes in bringing about the German re-occupation of the Rhineland in March 1936?

◆ Why didn't Britain and France take any serious action over Germany's re-occupation of the Rhineland in March 1936?

◆ Why was Hitler able to get away with the annexation of Austria in March 1938?

◆ Why were Britain and France not prepared to stop the German annexation of Austria in March 1938?

◆ *'Chamberlain tried his hardest to settle the Czechoslovakian Crisis of 1938 in a peaceful way.'* Does a study of Chamberlain's actions between April and October 1938 support this claim?

◆ Account for the different attitudes of Germany, Britain, France and Czechoslovakia in 1938 towards the Sudeten Crisis.

◆ What factors influenced the course of British foreign policy towards Czechoslovakia in 1938?

◆ *'Chamberlain's greatest triumph but Britain's greatest shame.'* Discuss this view of the Munich Settlement of September 1938.

◆ Why was the Czechoslovakian Crisis of 1938 so important in international relations?

◆ Why did Hitler want to conquer Poland?

◆ What were the main reasons for Britain appeasing Germany between 1933 and 1939?

◆ Why did Britain follow a policy of appeasement in the 1930s?

◆ *'It was a policy of both necessity and choice.'* Does this comment adequately explain why Britain followed a policy of appeasement in the 1930s?

EXAMPLE OF PLAN FOR EXTENDED RESPONSE

Why did Britain follow a policy of appeasement in the 1930s?

Introduction

Briefly outline meaning of appeasement. Indicate that there are several reasons which make sense as to why the policy was followed: Chamberlain's own attitudes, Military factors, British attitudes towards Germany and Treaty of Versailles, British concerns about its possible allies (Russia, France, USA), financial factors.

Chamberlain's own views

Hatred of war, worries of effect on civilians, 'bomber will always get through' mentality. Worried about losing elections if government spends money re-arming.

Military factors

Pessimistic information from CIGS, over-estimation of strength of German airforce, worries about Britain's Royal Navy being over-stretched.

British attitudes towards Germany and Treaty of Versailles

Long-term feeling that Versailles was wrong therefore give way to Germany, feeling that Eastern Europe was not Britain's business.

British concerns about its possible allies (Russia, France, USA, Empire and Commonwealth)

Why Britain couldn't/wouldn't make a pact with Communist Russia, attitudes towards France who was seen as weak, attitudes towards USA, seen as unreliable, concern with Empire as Britain's first duty, and where Commonwealth stood on supporting Britain over central European affairs.

Financial factors

Influence of Treasury on financial implications of intervening, effects of recent economic slump and need to spend scarce money on welfare improvements.

Conclusion

Clear that several factors had influence on why Britain followed a policy of appeasement. Since Chamberlain seemed to conduct British foreign policy and policy of appeasement almost by himself from 1937, then clearly Chamberlain's own attitudes were a key part of the explanation. However, he was operating within a framework of constraints, and the other factors also had influence at different times.

NOTE ON SOURCES

Historians rely on a variety of sources to find out about diplomatic developments in Europe between the wars. No teacher or pupil could be expected to study all of the following sources, but at different parts of the course, they all have a value in helping to make sense of the events. The following sections may also give you clues as to what sources you could investigate when you are preparing your extended response.

PRIMARY SOURCES

Official documents are a rich source of reference for studying British inter-war diplomacy. Speeches in parliament, the reports of CIGS and Minutes of Cabinet meetings all give a detailed coverage of responses to foreign events.

For the German point of view the Hossbach Memorandum, diplomatic reports and Hitler's speeches provide clues as to what the 'official' view was.

Newspapers can give a good impression of the public response to events. However, they should be studied with care. Too often they reported according to the prejudices of their editors/owners. *The Times* was very pro-appeasement (also the *Express* and *Mail*) while the *Mirror* and *Daily Herald* were generally anti-appeasement. The two top-selling Sunday newspapers (*People* and *News of the World*) couldn't make up their minds what view to consistently hold on appeasement!

Memoirs, diaries and letters from the main participants are always helpful in understanding their attitudes towards the events that they were helping to cause. They also help to provide examination setters with good sources for questions! Chamberlain was prepared to put a lot of his thoughts into his diary (as well as his regular letters to his sisters), and these are very revealing about his attitudes. Some of the historians listed below relied heavily on Chamberlain's diaries and letters (in the library of Birmingham University).

Winston Churchill's memoirs have also been prominent in helping to shape the way people viewed the Chamberlain years. In *The Second World War: Vol 1 The Gathering Storm* (Cassell 1948) Churchill helped reinforce the post-war view of Chamberlain as 'the guilty man'.

From the German point of view, Adolf Hitler's *Mein Kampf* (Pimlico) gives insights into his irrational way of thinking, but no (normal) pupil could seriously be expected to get into its 600 pages. Hitler's *Zweites Buch* (Secret Book) written in 1928, similarly helps to explain the workings of a deranged mind.

Cartoon collections are valuable in giving a visual and often ironic slant to the great diplomatic moments. Examination setters always enjoy putting in a good cartoon which often sums up the events neater than a paragraph of writing. Cartoons from Low, Shepard and Gabriel were especially perceptive and very critical of both Germany and the appeasement policy of the British government. You can see why Low (despite being a New Zealander) was on Hitler's list of people to be executed once he had conquered Britain! The best place to study these cartoons is the Internet site of the Centre for the Study of Cartoons and Caricature at the University of Canterbury at http://library.ukc.ac.uk/cartoons/

SECONDARY SOURCES

Books

Any booklist on Europe between the wars is likely to miss out as many good books as it includes! The following list includes some 'old faithfuls' that are as readable now as when they were first written, as well as newer studies. The first part of the list were not written with 16–17 year old pupils in mind, but (if still in print) are sometimes capable of being understood in small and careful doses.

C.L. Mowat	*Britain between the Wars*	Methuen	1955
A.J.P. Taylor	*The Origins of the Second World War*	Penguin	1961
J.W. Wheeler-Bennett	*Munich: A Prologue to Tragedy*	Macmillan	1964
William Carr	*Arms, Autarky and Aggression*	Edward Arnold	1972
William R Rock	*British Appeasement in the 1930s*	Edward Arnold	1977
Anthony Adamthwaite	*Making of the Second World War*	Allen and Unwin	1979
Frank McDonough	*Neville Chamberlain, Appeasement and the British Road to War*	Manchester University Press	1998
R.A.C. Parker	*Chamberlain and Appeasement*	Macmillan	1993
Alan Farmer	*British Foreign and Imperial Affairs 1919–39*	Hodder and Stoughton	1992

Books more suitable for students are:

Ruth Henig	*The Origins of the Second World War*	Routledge	1985
Andrew Boxer	*Appeasement*	Collins	1998
Alan Monger	*Causes of the Second World War*	Longman	1998
Ronald Cameron	*Appeasement between the Wars*	Pulse	1992
Keith Robbins	*Appeasement*	Historical Association	1988
Russell Stone	*The Drift to War*	Heinemann	1981
Josh Brooman	*Roads to War*	Longman	1989
David Adelman	*Signs of the Times*	Hodder and Stoughton	1991

(One very good section of 20 pages)

Chris Culpin and Ruth Henig	*Modern Europe 1870–1945*	Longman	1997

(One section of 20 pages ... very good on historiography)

Robert Pearce	*Contemporary Britain 1914–79*	Longman	1996

(One chapter of 13 pages)

Video programmes

The 1930s were the great age of the cinema newsreel with much original filmed footage of the great diplomatic moments. Many excellent TV documentaries have been made which incorporate historians' commentaries with the newsreel film. The best ones came out at the 50th anniversary of the Munich Settlement in 1988, and may still be around on video.

- Channel 4   *Peace in our Time*   198
- ITV   *Munich: The Peace of Paper*   198

Other reasonable programmes which cover much of the right ground are:

- BBC   History File – *The Drift to War: Causes of World War 2*   199
- BBC   The Wrong War – *Nazis: A Warning from history*   199
- Channel 4   *Did We have to Fight Hitler?*   199
- St Andrews University   199
  Video of sources for Appeasement and the Road to War to 1939

Internet

Some information on inter-war diplomacy and the leading statesmen can be found at different web-sites on the Internet. A word of warning though. History is **not** a subject where you just turn on, tune in, down load, print out, and hey presto, your work is done. Getting information off the Net is *just the start* of the study. To do history well there are no 'quick-fixes' or 'instant solutions', there is always the hard but satisfying graft of using and applying the knowledge and understanding you have to the questions or issues in hand. So, the Net can be useful in providing additional sources of information but it is not some sort of miracle cure.

Try using some of the educational web-sites to see if they include appeasement or International foreign policy information.

BBC Bitesize revision	http://www.bbc.co.uk/education/revision/gcsebitesize/history/index.shtml
BBC Education	http://www.bbc.co.uk/education/modern/roadwar/road/whtm.htm
Channel 4 education	http://www.channel4.com/nextstep/1939/
Grolier	http://gi.grolier.com/wwii/wwii_2.html
Mass Observation Archive	http://www.sussex.ac.uk/library/massobs/mohist.shtml
Public Records Office	http://www.pro.gov.uk/
History Today magazine	http://www.historytoday.com/help/index.cfm
The History Place	http://www.historyplace.com/worldwar2

Academic web-sites (often with an Americanised angle) include:
http://metalab.unc.edu/pha/
http://www.clearinghouse.net/cgi-bin/chadmin/viewcat/
Arts___Humanities/history?kywrd++

Glossary

appeasement	policy followed by British governments in the 1930s of favouring negotiation and concession with aggressive powers, to avoid having to go to war (see pages 78–79)
Armistice	11 November 1918; the day the fighting in the First World War stopped
Anschluss	Germany's take-over of Austria
Auslandsdeutsch	anyone with German ancestors, or who was German-speaking but, who lived outside Germany's 1930s borders
autonomy	separation from, leading to self rule
belligerent	warlike and aggressive
buffer zone	area between two unfriendly nations which may act as a buffer and absorb the shock of any conflict
Chancellor	like a prime minister; the head of the government
civilian	the part of the population that is still at home, *not* in the armed forces. Normally means the defenceless women and children
conscription	every male of a certain age would have to join the army for a certain period of time
constraint	a limit on how someone can behave; a restriction on their freedom of action
deranged	disturbed or upset
diplomacy	the conduct of foreign policy: the way nations deal with each other and react to each other's demands
equilibrium	balance, peacefulness or state of rest
evolutionary	taking things slowly and letting them evolve, rather than rushing things
expediency	behaving a certain way out of convenience; forgetting one's principles. Doing something because it seemed suitable in the circumstances and you could get away with it
Fuhrer	German for leader: Hitler's title as head of the German Reich
Gallup poll	a way of trying to work out public opinion by asking a sample of the population, and estimating what the total population might think
Great Depression	the economic slump of the early 1930s; a time of low industrial production and high unemployment
ideology	the set of beliefs that a political party has
Karlsbad Programme	the demands for autonomy by the Sudeten German Party in 1938
League of Nations	international peace-keeping organisation set up after the First World War, based in Geneva, Switzerland
Lebensraum	'living space': room to spread out needed for Germany's 'surplus' population
Maginot Line	line of French fortresses along their border with Germany
martial law	the use of military justice rather than civil law – armed forces patrol streets, curfews in operation
mediator	like a judge; someone who looks at the problem from both sides and tries to come up with a solution

Mein Kampf	book written by Hitler outlining his political views
mobilisation	the order that is given to put a country's armed forces at a state of war-readiness
mobilised	troops go to a state of war readiness, reserves are called up and war looks likely
Munich Putsch	Hitler's attempt to topple the German Government using force
nationalist	supporter of your own nation; wanting to build it up, believing it is better than other nations
neutrality	refusing to take side in any war; being neutral
non-aggression pact	where two countries promise not to fight each other
pacifist	lover of peace; someone who may refuse to fight or go to war
pact	a deal or an agreement between nations
parity in the air	an equal number of aeroplanes
plebiscite	like a referendum; a single question that the people are asked to vote on
Pravda	one of the official newspapers of the Russian government
programme	the set of policies of a political party
propaganda	giving information that will influence people to think a certain way
purged	killed, wiped out, removed from office
race	the different types or groups of people who live in the world (Slavs, Negroes, Caucasian etc.)
racism	favouring one race (group of people) due to the belief that it is superior to other races
rapprochement	French word meaning coming together in a better understanding of each other's ways of thinking; a growing friendship
ratify	to make a final decision over signing a treaty
Reich	German word meaning empire, but which usually just meant the German state
Reichstag	the German parliament which met in Berlin
Reichswehr	the small army that Germany was allowed after 1919; made much larger by Hitler after 1935 and renamed the *Wehrmacht*
repudiate	to cancel an agreement or refuse to obey a deal that had been made
revisionist	a) anyone who supported the German policy of wanting to revise the terms of the Treaty of Versailles b) a historian who wants to revise the earlier views on why Chamberlain ran his foreign policy the way he did
satellite state	a small state totally under the control of a neighbouring larger state
scaremongering	making things sound worse than they really are
territorial	matters to do with land or territory
ultimatum	a threat to take action unless certain conditions are met
unmitigated	something that cannot be excused, where nothing can be said in its favour
victuals	food – Churchill is referring to serving Hitler with all he wants

INDEX